The Vacation Rental Bible:

Proven Tips to Find, Manage & Market Vacation Rental Properties for Maximum Profit

By Dave Mencel

"The best time to plant a tree was 20 years ago. The second-best time is now."

-Ancient Chinese Proverb

Contents

Introduction   **1**

Managing a Vacation Rental   *1*

Defining Your Investment Goals   *4*

Chapter 1: Choosing a Property   **6**

General Considerations   *6*

Seasonality Considerations & Rental Potential   *10*

Convenience Considerations – Keeping it Simple   *12*

Competitive Landscape   *13*

State & Local Laws / Regulations   *15*

HOA Restrictions   *16*

Finally – Finding the Perfect Property   *17*

Chapter 2: Balancing Your Budget   **19**

Introduction to Budgeting   *19*

Costs of Entry, Setup & Furnishing: The Capital Budget   *21*

Reserve Accruals – Planning for Future Capital Expenditures   *25*

Building an Operating Budget   *28*

Play with Your Budget – And Stress Test It   *32*

Chapter 3: Building a Network of Resources   **35**

On-Site or Remote?   *35*

Marketing Resources   *37*

Co-Hosts & Other Resources   *40*

Cleaning Services   *42*

Handyman Services   *44*

Professional Property Management   *47*

Chapter 4: Getting Rental Ready   **49**

Choosing a Target Demographic   *49*

Furnishing: Where to Spend and Where to Skimp   *51*

Simplify Your Workflow with Technology   *56*

Creating a Welcome Guide   *59*

Chapter 5: Photography Tips to Make Your Listing Pop   **62**

DIY or Pro?   62

Staging the Space   63

Shooting   64

Lighting   70

Editing   73

Enhanced Marketing   76

Chapter 6: Creating & Maintaining Your Listing   **79**

Scoping out the Competition   79

Writing Compelling Marketing Copy   81

Writing Effective House Rules   86

Defining Your Booking Settings   89

Setting Your Pricing   92

Maintaining Your Listing   96

Using Feedback to Improve   97

Chapter 7: Marketing, SEO & and Growing Your Clientele   **102**

Organic Search Engine Optimization   102

Earning 5-Star Reviews   105

Superhost Status   107

Airbnb Plus Status   109

Friends & Family   109

Social Media & Other Marketing Channels   111

Chapter 8: Managing Your Guests   **113**

Operating like a Business   113

Taking Care of Your Guests   115

The Guest Isn't Always Right – Handling Difficult Guests   116

Chapter 9: Managing Income and Cashflow   **121**

Chapter 10: Exit & Contingency Planning   **129**

Conclusion   **134**

Glossary of Terms   **136**

Introduction

Managing a Vacation Rental

What do a corporate manager from Wisconsin, a retiree from Washington, a news reporter from Colorado, a realtor from Arizona and a middle-manager from New Mexico all have in common? They all manage very successful short-term rentals in the same condo complex where my wife and I bought our first vacation rental. And similar to us at the time, they all knew little to nothing about how to do it (with the possible exception of the realtor). But we all discovered that although managing a vacation rental takes time, dedication and a certain degree of patience, it's far from rocket science. With the right knowledge, property and pricing policies, anyone can do it successfully.

This book is a tool to guide you on your own journey of finding and managing a short-term vacation rental property. Whether your goal is to maximize profit, simply break-even on a place you already own or just make a few extra bucks off of a place where you already live, the tips you'll find here will apply equally well. Additionally, while this book most frequently references Airbnb, the topics and advice apply to any similar sites like HomeAway, Vrbo or even your professional property manager's website. We are in no way recommending any one site or marketing platform; we are simply referencing those you will most likely be using for your rental property.

For first-time investors looking to make their first vacation rental investment, this book can be read cover to cover as a step-by-step guide. For experienced investors or those that already own a property, each chapter in this book is designed to serve as a standalone reference to the topics it covers. Feel free to skip around; if you've already bought your place, you won't miss anything by skipping the *Choosing a Property* chapter. You can always come back to it when you're ready to buy your next place!

It's also important to note that this book focuses on *short-term* vacation rentals. While many of the tips apply equally well to monthly and longer term rentals, this book is focused on information specific to managing short-term rentals (one day to under one month) and will not delve into such topics as tenant rights, evictions, landlord insurance, vacancy insurance, Schedule E's and other topics frequently experienced by landlords (defined as those that are writing legal leases to host their guests). Additionally, this book is aimed at those that offer their guests a dedicated space, not a shared space. This could be your primary residence while you are not using it, it may be a vacation home you use a few weeks each year or it may be a home you've purchased exclusively as an investment property and will never sleep a single night in yourself. In any case, the advice you'll find here assumes that whenever your guests are in your space, you are not.

Finally, while we have significant experience in managing our own vacation rentals, we are not experts in tax law, GAAP accounting or your local laws. Use this book as a guide, but do not treat the specifics of what we discuss on these topics as gospel. In these areas of legal concerns, we are aiming to educate you as to what questions you should be asking, but it's your responsibility to ask these questions of a competent professional and validate their answers. As with any business endeavor, you should consult a reputable in-market CPA for tax-related questions and a business attorney for legal structure questions or interpretations of local laws.

Defining Your Investment Goals

The most important up-front consideration is understanding why you want to manage your own vacation rental. There are no wrong answers, but do take the time to reflect on this question and provide yourself an honest answer. How you answer the question will impact how you manage your rental property. This book is written with the assumption that your goal is to operate a successful rental *business* and to maximize long-term profitability. In other words, you are looking to maintain as close to 100% occupancy as possible with the highest nightly rate while minimizing expenses (but as you'll see, this does *not* mean scrimping), while simultaneously providing a 5-star level of service for your guests to ensure this revenue stream does not dry up.

If your goals are more modest, however, such as renting your primary residence while you're away, earning just enough income to support a hobby or even if you don't care about the financial piece and just enjoy the interaction with guests and making someone else's vacation a little more memorable, you'll find the steps required to achieve your goals are quite similar. After all, running a vacation rental is rather formulaic, like baking a cake; there's a little trial and error, but once you've discovered the recipe that works for you, all that's left to do is replicate and enjoy the benefits.

Formulaic does not mean easy, however. Yes, running a rental property is systematic and it's conceptually easy to manage a successful rental. It still involves a lot of time, hard work, dealing with people from various walks of life, handling the occasional frustrated guest, dealing with subcontractors like cleaners, handymen and plumbers, and experiencing situations that are generally beyond your control. If you stay in this business long enough, you will experience some or all of these issues, and at times you may wonder why you ever purchased a rental property. But you'll get through it and reap the rewards in the long term. This type of investing is not a get rich quick scheme, but done correctly, it can be a great get rich slow scheme, establishing a healthy stream of positive cashflow to supplement or replace your standard income for many years.

Chapter 1: Choosing a Property

General Considerations

The success of your vacation rental will depend on many factors, but the old adage "Location, Location, Location" may arguably sum up the most important success factor for determining the maximum rental revenue potential for your property. If your property isn't in an area that can support a vacation rental, no amount of efforts on your part will keep occupancy at an optimum level that justifies the time and money you will invest into your rental business. This isn't to say that occupancy is the only critical factor in profitability, but location will definitely set an expectation for the maximum you should expect to earn. We've even seen markets where an 800 square foot condo is fetching almost the same nightly rental rate as 2,300 square foot homes. The driving force behind price is supply and demand. Just as in traditional macroeconomics, supply and demand drive market pricing, and popular vacation destinations are generally short on vacation rentals in peak seasons, making other factors (like price) less relevant.

Of course, most markets will not exhibit such price inelasticity to the extreme mentioned above, at least not throughout the year, but we do see that location is generally the dominant driver of market prices, potential occupancy and thus potential revenue. Being a Superhost, providing 5-star service, having wonderful reviews, investing in top notch furnishings and other factors are important prerequisites to realizing the maximum potential in that market, but these factors don't really serve to increase the maximum possible revenue. To put it differently, location is the primary factor that determines the size of the revenue pie. All other factors determine how many slices of that pie you get to eat and how many will go to your competition instead. Of course, this isn't true in all markets, but it holds true in most vacation markets. Location will be discussed more thoroughly later, so bear with us for the moment.

Let's outline the other factors that affect profitability. We've mentioned that location drives rental revenue, or top line earnings. But profitability – the difference of revenue minus expenses – is really what we care about. Therefore, to maximize profitability in a market where we are assuming maximum revenue is predominantly fixed by location, it makes sense that we should minimize expenses in order to maximize profitability. "Expenses" is a very broad category that will be broken down in greater detail in the next chapter, but we'll start with a quick high-level overview of budgeting to help understand the types of expenses that drive your vacation rental. Specifically, your capital budget and your operating budget are the tools you'll use to estimate your rental property's potential profitability. While both are important, the main factor in determining your up-front expenses will be your capital budget: the cost to acquire, renovate (if needed) and furnish the home to make it rental-ready. The operating budget consists of your ongoing maintenance expenses such as cleanings, replenishing toiletries and replacing or repairing broken or damaged items. Operating expenses loosely correlate to the square footage of the property and don't tend to vary much from market to market, at least not within the continental United States, since the cost of bed sheets is the same wherever you are, electricity and internet don't vary wildly from location to location and so on.

We'll delve into developing reliable budgets in *Chapter 2*, so for now just know that your capital budget consists of the cost to acquire a property and make it ready for your first guests. If minimizing upfront (or capital) expenses is the goal, it follows that finding a less expensive property is prudent. This may mean less square footage, a fixer-upper or a less desirable (secondary) location. It is important to note that any less desirable location you choose should still be an *overall* desirable location; do not confuse it with an *undesirable* location. For example, one of our first properties was in the Village of Oak Creek just south of Uptown Sedona in Arizona. Uptown is *the* place to be, but the Village of Oak Creek is quieter, closer to the Phoenix airport and generally a wonderful place for people to start and end their daily journey into the downtown areas and hiking/biking trails. Most importantly from an investor's point of view, the Village of Oak Creek is significantly less expensive to buy into but retains *most* of the rental potential of the downtown area. It's a sound business strategy to sacrifice a little bit of revenue in order to have a drastic reduction in expenses as long as the benefits outweigh the negatives. There is a definite limit to the effectiveness of this method, however. Move even one more town away past the Village of Oak Creek, and property values stay similar but vacation rental revenue potential plummets. This is perhaps wonderful for owner-occupied homes and long-term rentals, but not great for vacation rental investors.

Assuming you will use a traditional combination of down payment plus financing to pay for the property, then it's likely that the largest expense you'll have is actually acquiring the property. After this, there may be renovations to make the property suitable for guests (especially if you bought a fixer-upper), and then there is the large upfront expense of furnishing the property. These latter two expenses will vary from property to property, but your goal is to spend wisely so you minimize your outlay without scrimping on the items your guests need for enjoyment or safety. An important aside to consider is that how you choose to furnish your property may be affected by other factors such as your own use of the property. As a personal example, my wife and I will spend our money very differently renovating a property we plan to use ourselves occasionally versus renovating a property we plan to exclusively rent. I enjoy cooking, so you'll find a more modern and complete kitchen in a property we use, and a more modest kitchen in a property we don't. But we don't spend more in these cases with profitability in mind; we do it for our personal enjoyment and are willing to let profitability drop a little. This is a balance each investor needs to determine before purchasing a property.

It's difficult to give specific guidance on fixer-uppers versus turnkey properties because many of the decisions will depend on how much of the work you do yourself. As a general rule of thumb, if you will do the renovation work yourself, a fixer-upper could be a great value, but if you will hire a general contractor to oversee your renovation, you may find a better deal by buying a turnkey property, especially as your first investment. However, if you will use the property personally for a significant amount of time, getting exactly what you want through renovations may be worth it. In the end, it's a personal decision for you to make; the budget templates included in *Chapter 2* can help you make your choice.

After your property has been renovated, all that's left to spend from your capital budget is the cost of furnishings. The cost to furnish will vary roughly with square footage, with a multiplier for the style you choose. A modestly furnished two-bedroom, 1,000 square foot condo may cost $10,000 to furnish modestly and $15,000 to furnish higher-end. A two-bedroom, 2,000 square foot condo will cost approximately double that, and so on. You can easily see why a smaller property is more ideal for a vacation rental in a market where both of these condos fetch fairly similar rental rates. I'll take 10% less rental revenue any day at a property that costs half as much to set up and operate – and you should too!

Finally, we will comment briefly on the operating budget. The operating budget consists of the day-to-day expenses to keep your rental running smoothly: electricity, heat, water, HOA fees, internet, cable, toiletries, minor repairs and replacements, marketing and so on. While there are steps you can take to minimize these expenses (for example, smart thermostats may limit your heat and air conditioning expense), the cost savings will generally be minimal and, in many cases, these expenses are beyond your normal control and fall into the category we refer to as the cost of doing business. Yes, it is prudent to minimize these expenses when possible, but I generally don't worry too much about them when *choosing* a rental property (HOA fees perhaps being the notable exception, as these can vary wildly within a locale). Once the property is up and running, the capital expenses become sunk costs and the operating budget becomes the driving management tool. The operating budget will become of more importance later on as the capital budget becomes more of a secondary concern.

Seasonality Considerations & Rental Potential

Location has been discussed as the primary driving force in determining your rental revenue, but depending on the location you choose, a high *seasonal* revenue may be sufficient to make a decent profit. For example, let's consider the mountain town of Kalispell, Montana outside of Glacier National Park. This area sees peak activity for less than half of the year, yet the market has been designed around this; the market generally supports maintaining a profitable rental with only 50% occupancy, give or take. Since the peak occupancy window is very short, it becomes critical to make sure you get as much occupancy as you can during the short season. You need 100% occupancy during the *peak* season in markets like this. This means same-day turns, one-night minimums to fill gaps, etc. Depending on the particular supply and demand forces at play in your specific market, this may be very easy to achieve (or not so easy). In a market truly short of vacation rental housing, you will have no problem achieving this. By bringing your property to market, you actually make the vacation rental revenue pie bigger, and you can easily carve your own piece from this now larger pie. However, in a market already saturated with rentals, you won't add to the pie, you'll just be fighting for your piece. As discussed above, this is where 5-star service can help differentiate you and your property.

Discussing the peak season is important because it's where most of your revenue will be made, but even more interesting to discuss is the off-season. If you run your rental well, and are able to fill it with either a higher than average occupancy or rental rate (or both) during the off-season, something almost magical can happen: you can make a lot of profit quickly. You've taken a property that's meant to produce income operating nominally for a fraction of the year and expanded it to operate during a larger portion of the year.

If you design your budget to produce profit after renting for 25 weeks per year, and you find you can actually rent for 26 weeks at nearly the same rate, your revenue would be approximately 4% higher. Not bad for one extra week! If many of your expenses are fixed, that extra 4% is then mostly profit. Achieving this isn't easy. I guarantee you that every host in the area wants to achieve the same scenario, and in the off-season, the size of the pie is very small. You need to become an expert at claiming as large a piece as you can. In these markets, you will need effective sales and marketing, excellent reviews and an overall strong reputation to make it happen, but it can be wonderful to achieve!

Finally, it's worth noting that even in highly seasonal markets, the specific property location is still a very important consideration. Returning to the Kalispell/Glacier National Park example, if your property is right next to the national park's main entrance, you'll likely see a higher rental rate than if you're on the south side of Kalispell where the drive to the park gate may be 45 minutes. In this case, the *macro* factors of location determine that you will see a large seasonality effect, while the *micro* factors of location (e.g., distance to the Glacier National Park entrance) determine your revenue potential during the peak season. Being closer to the park means higher revenue but likely also incurs higher expenses in the form of higher property costs. You need to determine which location maximizes overall profitability best. The budgets in *Chapter 2* can help you do exactly that.

Convenience Considerations – Keeping it Simple

Keeping it simple means making it easy for both you and for your guests. These two considerations may be substantially different – or not. For example, keeping it simple for you may mean purchasing a property within a two-hour driving distance so you can be on site quickly in an emergency. Your guests don't care where you live permanently, so it's of no consideration to them. Their expectation already dictates they'll get help in an emergency. Instead, your guests' needs focus on considering the proximity to main attractions in the area, freeways or the nearest grocery store or Starbucks.

If you use the property yourself, it's possible that your needs and your guests' needs are one and the same. It's not essential that your needs align, but it's very nice when they do because there are fewer overall factors to consider when choosing a property. Even if your needs don't align, you can still find properties that keep life simple for both you and your guests; it may just take a bit more work or expense on your part. For example, for our out-of-state properties, we rely heavily on keeping the entire property internet connected to smart devices, giving us the ability to lock/unlock the front door, adjust the temperature, turn on/off lights remotely and check wireless router status. This is easy to accomplish but is more expensive than purchasing traditional products. It is ultimately great for us and our guests and meets both of our needs well.

12

For your first vacation rental, we recommend that you keep it simple for yourself as much as possible. For *every* vacation rental venture, we recommend keeping it easy for your guests. You can add complexity for yourself with future properties as it suits you (for example, purchasing an out-of-state property that you can use or a remote cabin location because it gives your guests a unique wilderness experience). These properties can be very rewarding to host and own (especially if you use them yourself), but they definitely offer unique complexities compared to the rental you can drive to in an hour and that's right down the road from a Home Depot.

Competitive Landscape

Once you've narrowed down the location for your investment, especially at the macro level (state, town or city), but also at the micro level (neighborhood or street), you should begin a deep competitive analysis. Fortunately, Airbnb, Vrbo and local property management companies make this very easy to do, though it is a bit time consuming. These are some of the key factors you will want to explore:

• What rates are others charging?

• What are occupancy rates for homes that appear to be exclusively rentals (ones that the owners don't use for their own vacations)?

• What are others charging for cleaning fees?

• Are others charging extra-guest or other miscellaneous fees?

• Are others allowing pets, and what is the pet fee?

• Is there a typical minimum number of nights that a typical host allows?

You can quickly create an account on each of the popular vacation rental sites, and shop around for the above information about homes in your chosen area. Examining this data will give you an idea of the revenue you can expect in a similar situation. Benchmark only 5-star hosts. You don't want to be anything less than 5-star yourself, and lower service levels will impact rental revenue.

It is also important to examine, both online and in person, how other property owners are furnishing their spaces. If the property you're looking at isn't in your area, stay in some competitive units when you go out to visit; don't stay in hotels. Make a note of how the properties feel, whether the furnishings are high-end, low-end or in the middle, and any aspects of the stay that really appealed to you or that you really disliked. Much of this information can be found online as well by searching Airbnb and equivalent sites, noting the pricing structure of comparable rentals and reviewing the photographs provided. The information you gain will help you to plan your own furnishing budget as you prepare to run your profitability analyses.

Finally, if you're looking to purchase within a multi-unit condo complex, talk to other hosts in the complex and ask about their successes. You can learn the most by simply asking someone that has done it already, and you'll find most people are willing to share their details if you approach them politely and honestly. This is especially true when they have a system that works very well; if they're confident in their own methods, they won't view you as a serious competitive threat. When my wife and I were searching for our first rental property, multiple owners in the complex where we ended up purchasing a home were willing to screenshot their progress, including occupancy percentages and annual revenue, to share with us. This was immensely helpful in creating our budgets! It's important to note that in our particular market there was a drastic shortage of vacation rentals and demand far exceeded supply, so none of us were competing strongly; in a different business environment, that type of information may not have been shared so willingly.

State & Local Laws / Regulations

Never overlook the importance of state and local laws. Arizona for example had a statewide ban on rentals of less than 30 days (short-term rentals) until just a few years ago, but now the vacation rental market there is booming. Some states require that you register as a landlord or rental company or obtain a business license. Other states have no restrictions provided you pay your taxes and operate legally. It is important to research these laws, as some states may not be worth the headache, even if the numbers make sense. Other states may be logistically easy for you, but too expensive and kill your budget before you even begin. It is important to understand the laws even down to the city level. Think a New York City vacation rental makes sense? Think again – NYC is one of the most regulated vacation rental markets in the country.

Before you commit to purchasing a property, *know the laws*. Your realtor will be a great resource in this regard; find one that specializes in selling rentals and ideally vacation rentals. Reach out to a few owners on Airbnb or HomeAway. You'll likely find most (but not all) are willing to share experiences and lessons learned. It's a friendly community where everyone can learn from each other. But a word to the wise: advice is cheap, but it's not always good. Verify everything yourself with someone trained to provide advice in that area – be it a realtor, lawyer or CPA, depending on the topic. Ultimately, you are responsible for your own actions!

In most cases, you'll learn that you can set up a vacation rental with only a few minor hoops to jump through – be it a legal structure, an operating permit, a tax license or some other registration paperwork to fill out. But it's your responsibility to the entire

15

vacation rental owner community to ensure you operate within the boundaries of the law.

HOA Restrictions

Homeowner associations, or HOAs, are organizations that make and enforce rules for the properties and their residents in condos, planned communities and some subdivisions. HOAs can be difficult roadblocks to the vacation market, or they can be wholly supportive of the endeavor. Do your research prior to purchasing a property with an HOA. Obtain the CC&Rs (Covenants, Conditions & Restrictions) and R&Rs (Rules and Regulations), and make sure you understand them. Know how the HOA is governed. Try to meet the Board of Directors and find out if they (or anyone else) are also using the property for vacation rentals. In some cases, significant investor ownership can make it difficult to obtain financing for a property (many of these loans are non-warrantable), so talk to your bank early to confirm they will finance the property; otherwise, prepare to find alternate funding methods. Ironically, properties that don't finance simply because they're in predominantly investor-owned communities often can be wonderful purchases despite being tougher to acquire and subsequently sell. Having a majority investor-owned community means you're all like-minded and aligned to a common goal; the community will behave for the good of the investors, which is very different than a community behaving for the benefit of the residents.

If your HOA does allow short-term rentals to operate, try to determine how this is governed. Is it allowed simply because it hasn't been banned? Or is it explicitly stated in your governing documents that short-term rentals are allowed? The former can be regulated quickly, the latter may take more effort. If it is explicitly allowed, are there any fees to operate a vacation rental, and in which specific documents is it allowed? If it's in your R&Rs, it may be very easy for the condo board to remove the right to operate a vacation rental with a simple board vote. If it's in your CC&R documentation, it's very difficult and expensive for your HOA to take away the right to operate short-term rentals. The latter is very desirable for you as an investor and a likely sign that there may be quite a few investors in your community already. If there is no documented provision, be wary and do your due diligence first. Attend a few board meetings and ask questions about short-term rentals. The answers you get should be insightful as to where the board stands on the topic. If you do purchase into one of these communities, have a backup plan. If your HOA suddenly bans vacation rentals, what's your next step? Can you still offer monthly rentals, and does this still make sense financially for you?

Finally – Finding the Perfect Property

You've done your research. You've made a preliminary budget, and the numbers look great. You've talked to a realtor, and they have a property that meets your criteria and fits your budget. It may or may not need fixing up, but if it does, it's well within your competency or you have a great general contractor lined up already. You've run countless financial analyses, and in every case you're happy with the numbers. The property will finance. You have the down payment. The HOA CC&R's are vacation rental-friendly. You can see your rental guests being very happy there, and as a plus, you can see your own family enjoying the property one or two weeks per year. Now what?

Depending on where you live and how your state governs real estate transactions, your next step is likely to make an offer. This is particularly true in states that have an open inspection period for a property with a cancelation for any reason. If this is your state, don't overthink it; write the offer. If you live in a less lenient state for canceling a transaction, you may need to do a bit more due diligence up front and make sure you're 100% committed. You may only be able to get out of the transaction if your home inspector finds a defect that the seller won't remedy.

Negotiating the deal and understanding your state and local laws is well beyond the scope of this book, but that's why you're working with a real estate agent. They can help you to pick the best starting price for negotiation to end up at a deal both you and the seller can live with.

We're often asked why more people aren't snagging properties immediately if they're a good deal. If the place I've found is so wonderful, why has it been on the market for 60 days? Wouldn't a savvier investor have snapped it up already? Sometimes, that's just the way it is. Sometimes no one knows the reason. Perhaps the seller was asking too much and after three low offers they realized they're overpriced. Sometimes different eyes see different potential. Sometimes you just get lucky. But luck can run out. If you've found the right property, buy it. After all, you only live once!

One final note: we've seen countless transactions get sidelined by a few thousand dollars. Sometimes you can't negotiate the purchase price you want. Sometimes you can't get the seller to credit you for the failing HVAC unit or the 18-year-old hot water heater that's leaking. Use your judgment. This is business, and business is never perfect. Sometimes you just have to swallow your pride and think to yourself "One more week of rental revenue and I can cover that water heater myself." Don't let a good deal pass by just because it isn't the perfect deal. With every property we own, including our own personal residence, I can think of at least three things I wish I had done differently after writing the offers. But since our property investments are cash flowing, so it's a moot point.

Chapter 2: Balancing Your Budget

Before reading this chapter, please download the supplemental Excel budget template from the following link:

bit.ly/vacationrentalbible

Introduction to Budgeting

When you purchase a vacation rental unit and if you plan to self-manage, you're essentially buying yourself a job. This is not a long-term rental where one tenant may stay for years and you work a month or so in between tenants, and it is definitely not a share of stock some CEO will manage for you. When you purchase a vacation rental, *you* are the CEO that will manage it; you are putting yourself right into an active management spot in the vacation rental business. This means a significant investment in your time and a very significant investment in your capital – the money you've worked hard to grow throughout your lifetime. It makes sense to spend some upfront time on due diligence to make sure you're making a prudent investment.

Luckily, budgeting for a single vacation rental property is straightforward and formulaic work. Like other upfront aspects of this business, it can be rather time consuming, but it's easy enough that anyone can do it. But budgeting does demand a certain level of attention to detail; get it wrong, and you can end up sitting on an asset that's costing you money instead of making you money.

Before going any further, we recommend one more quick self-assessment before we dive into the financials:

1. Is vacation rental management work you want to do or that you are willing to do?

2. Will you still be willing to do the work after three years? After seven years?

3. If you answered yes to both of the above, ask yourself again. Are you sure?

The timelines in the questions above are purpose-built. For most properties we have evaluated, if you were to you give up the property in the first three years, you would likely not break even. This literally means you would have lost money. The cost to renovate and furnish is never recouped, and the commission to sell will likely outweigh your earnings given that your property hasn't had much time to appreciate. If you give up in years four to seven, you will probably recoup your expenses and likely even make a little money, but not enough to justify the four to seven years' worth of work (unless you value your time well below minimum wage). But if you hang in there for the long term, you'll develop an asset that has paid back the initial capital investment while also providing a stable cashflow for many, many years to come. That's where the real payoff is. To repeat this book's introduction, a vacation rental is *not* a get rich quick deal, but it *may* be a good get rich slow plan if well executed.

One final caveat before we begin building the budget: the budget in this book is *not* a tax guide. It's a planning tool for determining if your property will be profitable or not. The budgets developed in this book do not calculate your income the same way the IRS would for tax purposes, because certain non-cash expenses like depreciation are intentionally omitted, and certain non-deductible expenses like mortgage principle are intentionally included. Our budgets are used only to determine if a rental will be profitable. Tax strategy is beyond the scope of this book. Taxation and tax strategy will be affected by changing federal, state and local laws. This important topic is best left to a qualified local CPA. A knowledgeable CPA, especially if you've never hired one, should easily pay for themselves quickly in the tax savings you'll realize.

Costs of Entry, Setup & Furnishing: The Capital Budget

Before we dive into creating a budget, we'll preface that this chapter is about building an overall picture of expected financial performance and financial health of your rental. Therefore, this chapter will focus on building annual budgets and will not drill down to the level of monthly budgeting. In *Chapter 9*, we'll focus on managing cashflow; *Chapter 9* takes the budgets created here to the next level with monthly projections that help to manage your income, smooth out your operations and time your cash withdrawals with more savvy. The monthly budgets are quite tactical in nature and represent an intended action plan. At this stage of your investment, you're simply looking to validate if an investment is a sound one and prepare for your initial purchase of a rental. If you've already purchased a property, you'll complete a high-level overview of its potential financial performance.

We'll consider two main budgets (capital and operating) that work together to form a complete picture of the financial health of your rental. The capital budget comes into play anytime you make a major investment into your property such as acquiring the property, improving the property or furnishing the property. There are no real sources of income in the capital budget, only expenses. In a business, these are your startup costs and subsequent cash infusions. You could argue that taking out a loan would be income into the capital budget, but for our purposes, income is limited to what your renters pay. Capital expenses are generally non-recurring and usually big-ticket items. They are sometimes forecastable but can at other times be unpredictable. For example, your water heater should last six to 10 years, but it may fail after three. The fact you eventually had to replace one shouldn't surprise you, but the accelerated timing might.

You should try your best to plan for the capital expenses (with your own reserve study– more on this later), and you should routinely accrue cash from your operating budget to put towards these eventual expenses. When you first purchase your property, you will have no guests and no income, so this cash will need to come from somewhere. Typically, you will need a combination of life savings and a mortgage, but it could also come from equity in another property or other various sources. Additionally, your cash reserves may not be fully funded by your income at the early stages. Say for example you need a $5,000 furnace in two years. It's unlikely you'll have accumulated enough cash from your normal reserves to pay for this, so early on you may need to make additional cash investments into your rental business to keep it running; with good planning you'll recoup these later on.

In the template, we divide the capital budget into three distinct areas: acquisition costs, renovation costs and furnishing costs. Acquisition costs are very straightforward and can often be estimated extremely well without much help or time from the moment you lay eyes on the property. These costs include:

• Acquisition cost of the property (purchase price)

• Lender fees, such as mortgage points, loan origination charges and other closing costs

• HOA fees (one-time property transfer fees and other fees excluding your monthly HOA assessment)

- Title insurance (insurance your mortgage holder may require to protect them against claims against the property's title)

- Business/legal fees (if you intend to hold the property in an LLC or hire a lawyer for the closing)

Renovation costs are probably the hardest to estimate in the capital budget and consist of things you will need to do today as well as things you will need to do down the road. The former represents a cash expense, and the latter represents a cash accrual. You will begin planning for the future expenses the day you start making revenue.

Renovations may not be required at all when you purchase the property turnkey, or extensive work may be needed to make it habitable if you've purchased a fixer-upper. Extensive work can be very difficult to estimate, but generally you will have a period of time to inspect a new property prior to closing. Walking the property with a general contractor is a good idea if you are considering a fixer-upper. Other ways to estimate renovation costs are by talking to contractors and realtors, and visiting stores like Home Depot or Lowe's (especially if you plan to do it yourself). Since the authors have no idea what you will need to do or want to do to your specific property in terms of renovations, nor do we know the local economics of your market (such as labor costs), this is one area where we are unable to offer you specific numbers to consider. You will have to determine your renovation costs on your own. When you have done so, you can enter the amount into the Excel worksheet "Planning Budget" under "Initial Renovations".

While we can't help with predicting your upfront renovation costs, we can help with predicting future capital expenses, like replacing a furnace or air conditioner. For a small property, you can easily complete your own reserve study to help estimate this, and we'll get to that in a moment. If you're not familiar with reserve studies, these are tools condo boards use to determine how to set their budgets, and you can easily do the same for your own. A reserve study employs an expert to assess the age and condition of key features of your property (e.g., roof, HVAC and plumbing), estimate the useful life remaining and replacement cost and give you guidance on how much you need to accrue to have the cash on hand when you need it to replace each asset. A well-run condo board will make sure the reserve account has enough money to ensure these replacements can be paid when needed. A poorly run condo board will charge special assessments or simply delay needed replacements. In your case, you can use it as a tool to see how much cash to keep in the business for when big-ticket items come due for replacement. While paying for these items is considered part of your capital expenses, the amount to set aside in reserves each month will come from your operating budget. That means that a small portion of your profit will be set aside each month and used to fund a separate business account that can be used for future capital expenses. Therefore, although these are capital expenses, we'll discuss them in the operating expense section since that's where the funding comes from.

Finally, the last item on your capital budget is furnishing. For many, this is the most fun budget to develop because you get to shop for the fun things you probably don't even have in your own home or haven't replaced in years. The Excel template has a dedicated tab for furnishings, and it's pre-filled in with the most common furnishings you'll need to purchase for each room listed on the spreadsheet based on our own experiences with furnishing. You only need to make any additions or subtractions from the list and estimate your own costs. You should have some idea of how you want to furnish – high end, low end, or something in between. Since your goal is to minimize expenses, and rental items tend to take abuse, we generally recommend aiming for lower to middle end and spending your money on more durable items that will last longer. To develop an estimate, just shop; go to your favorite stores, Home Depot, Ikea, Bob's Discount, or even surf Craigslist, eBay, or other similar sites. You don't have to furnish with brand-new furniture for it to look nice. Your guests know they're not the first ones in the space, so they expect a used condition anyways. Just don't buy junk and make sure any used items you purchase are in good to very good condition.

When you have completed filling in the Excel sheet with your furnishings, the total furnishings amount from the "Furnishings" tab will carry over into the "Planning Budget" tab. If you've followed the order listed in this book, that means your capital expense budget should be complete. You can read the line "TOTAL CAPITAL SPEND". That's how much actual cash you'll need to put into your property to get it ready for your first guest. In other words, you'll need to spend that much before you even begin to think about recouping a cent. If the number seems too high, you'll need to find alternate financing arrangements, a less expensive property or less expensive furnishings, or you'll have to cut back on your up-front renovations. If the number seems acceptable, then it's time to move on to operating expenses.

Reserve Accruals – Planning for Future Capital Expenditures

Before we get to the operating budget, we'll first elaborate on reserve accruals since it touches upon both the operating and capital expense budget. The idea behind a reserve budget is to begin allocating money from your operating income to be held in your business until you need it for major capital expenses. In your planning budget, these expenses will not show up in your capital budget because they happen in the future – sometime after you've purchased your property. They do show up in your operating expense. Think about it this way: if you think you need to purchase a $1,200 water heater one year from the day you purchase the property, you should be saving $100 per month for the first year of operations to have the money available when the purchase is needed.

Many property owners of both short-term and long-term rentals don't bother with budgeting for these replacements. They just deal with them as they happen from their personal budgets. This can put a strain on your personal budget, and if funds aren't available in your personal budget at the time, it can cause a needed repair to go unfixed for much longer than it should. With a long-term tenant, you may be able to get away with waiting a few weeks to replace the A/C in a hot summer, but that same few weeks with vacation renters in summer can mean half a dozen negative reviews in a row, which can be more costly than just replacing the A/C would have been. Finally, neglecting to plan for these items in your budget upfront will also cause you to overestimate the financial performance of your property. What you think is a 10% return on cash may in fact be a 2% return on cash when you factor in the aging mechanicals. Many people combine these reasons as well, arguing that since they will pay for repairs out of pocket when the time comes, it doesn't affect the "profitability" of their rental since it will cash flow. Nothing could be further from the truth! Spend the time and determine your reserve accruals.

To determine your reserve accrual amount, use the "Reserve Accruals" tab in the included Excel template. Add or remove any items to accurately reflect what you expect to replace on your home based on how it's built and what parts of it you are responsible for. Your list may look significantly different than ours since ours was made for a small cedar-sided house in Wisconsin. Similarly, tweak the asset life of each item. Different items last longer or shorter in different areas of the country. Your realtor or home inspector should be able to estimate replacement costs for many of the items on the list, and they likely can even recommend items to add to the list for your area. You don't need a firm quote for anything (unless that asset is due for immediate repair – but then it belongs in your renovation budget). Working with rough ballpark estimates is perfectly okay; you'll already be miles ahead of most investors just by going through this exercise. Because the overall dollar amounts can grow pretty quickly, if you forget a few items or poorly estimate a few items, it won't really matter much to the final dollar amount.

What we won't attempt to do in this book is to time these expenses; this is something you need to determine based on the specifics of your property. For example, if you have a roof, all appliances and your HVAC all due for replacement in your fifth to sixth year of home ownership, you'll need save more aggressively in these first five years than this spreadsheet will indicate since you'll need the money much sooner. You can modify the spreadsheet to add some columns for remaining service life and determine how much money you'll need each year, but this analysis is beyond the scope of this book and the included template.

One final thing to note: if your rental is a condo, you won't have to do much accrual planning compared to those with single-family detached homes. Your HOA will cover most items, while you'll just have to worry about what happens inside your walls, mainly paint, HVAC, plumbing and furnishings. Your HOA is likely required to complete a professional reserve study every few years that takes into account the timing of each major expense, and your condo board will use that to help structure your condo dues payments to make sure you're budgeting for these items. If well managed, you shouldn't have any special assessments when the time comes to replace an asset. Special assessments are one-time additional fees an HOA bills to the condo owners for major expenses when the HOA doesn't have the funds to do pay themselves. Most HOA's aren't fully funded, so it's probable you'll experience at least one special assessment during your ownership period if you hold the property long enough. Periodically hold discussions with your condo board to determine if they think any special assessments may be charged in the near future, and if so, add this to your accrual planning.

Building an Operating Budget

The operating budget is the day-to-day expenses you incur to keep the rental, well, operating. It also includes your income from renters. Most importantly, the operating budget is the tool that determines monthly or annual profitability and how much cash you can pull out of the property as owner's profit. The operating budget works together with the capital budget to determine the property's key financial performance metrics such as payback and return on cash. While the capital budget is the "big expenses," the operating budget is the "day to day" expenses, and the two come together to show overall performance.

The operating budget should be a living document that's updated periodically. We typically start a new one for each property for each tax year. Some items in the operating budget are easy to determine perfectly every time (your cable/internet and HOA dues, for example); others will require estimating to develop and can be refined over time as you improve your knowledge of that property and develop a history to draw on (electric/heat, repairs, travel, etc.). Items to consider in the operating budget include:

• Mortgage payment (principle + interest)

• HOA dues

• Internet / Cable

• Heat / Electricity

• Maintenance

• Repairs

• Guest amenities (toiletries, etc.)

• Marketing

• Travel (if your rental is remote, budget for yourself to be on site several times per year)

- Property management

- Trash collection

- Reserve accruals

- Property tax

- Insurance

- Legal fees (LLC, CPA, etc.)

To build your operating budget in Excel, use the "Planning Budget" tab in the downloadable template. The top of this sheet, capital expenses, should already be complete. The next two sections "Operating Budget – Expenses" and "Operating Budget – Income" are the key inputs. We've prepopulated the list with some of the most common experiences our properties experience, and we've left a few "Other" categories you can adjust as you see fit. Feel free to add or remove rows to suit your own needs. The sheet is set up for you to enter monthly budgeting information in the yellow cells. The template will calculate the annual amounts for you. The workbook will also calculate your mortgage payment for you automatically using information from the capital budget above, so double check the capital budget is complete.

When you have entered all of your planned expenses, it's time to move on to what is arguably the toughest part of the budget yet to estimate: your revenue. Fortunately, if you've done your competitive homework by studying other similar properties on Vrbo, Airbnb, HomeAway and others, or if you've spoken to other property owners in the area that have shared their information with you, or if you've discussed this with any local property managers, you should have enough to get you by. Pick your occupancy, pick your average nightly rental rate and enter any management fees that come off of the top (for example, if you've retained the help of a professional property manager), and Excel takes care of the rest.

When both income and expense are completed in the operating budget, and the capital budget is also complete, the final outputs of the total budget are the three key financial metrics that let you understand how your property is performing.

1. Net Rental Income: This is your annual operating profit after covering all of your expenses. Operating profit neglects your capital spending. It's very important to mention that this is not related to your net income for tax purposes, so do not use this budget to complete your tax return. Net rental income is the amount of cash you can take out of the business and put into your wallet to spend elsewhere. If this number is negative, that's your first red flag. A negative net income means money will be coming out of your pocket to keep this rental running. You're not getting paid for your time to manage the property; you're instead paying for the privilege to do it. Keep in mind that if you have a mortgage, then your guests are paying for it, not you. Additionally, you're putting some money away every month into a reserve accrual account for big-ticket expenses down the road, so it's not to say that your net rental income is the totality of cash the business has produced. Rather, it's the total cash the business has produced beyond its own needs to self-sustain. There is no set guideline on what a good number should be, because it can depend very heavily on the property and the terms under which it was purchased (financed versus all cash, etc.), and the owner's own goals. Personally, I'm happy if a property puts $1,000 in my pocket every month in the peak season and sits just above break-even in the slow season, but that works for us with the types of properties we purchase and our personal investment philosophy.

2. Payback Period: This metric refers to the amount of time until the operating income has fully "repaid" the initial capital expenses. In other words, if you put $100,000 out of pocket into acquiring and preparing the property for guests, how many years will it be until you've made $100,000 in net income from the property? Note, this is *not* at all related to paying off the property's mortgage and owning it free any clear. In fact, if you've put a ton of cash down on the property or paid in full in cash for the property, your payback will likely be a much longer term than if you put zero down on the property with a long term loan. In fact, in most cases you'll pay back your cash investment long before you pay off any mortgage. But that's okay because you're not paying your mortgage, your guests are, so don't worry about it! Again, payback varies heavily depending on how a property is financed, but assuming you've done a typical 20% down / 80% financed transaction with a 15-year loan, a decent payback is 5 to 10 years. Any shorter and you have a great looking property. Any longer and you may want to rethink your methods. First, what changes can you make to your strategy to improve the payback period, and second, if you can't change your strategy enough to make it work, do you expect some capital appreciation of the property in the 10-year timeframe that can offset your marginal payback? This is a bit of a riskier venture, and I generally never advise purchasing a vacation rental strictly for the hope of capital appreciation. For a deal that is marginal (but not poor) on payback, however, it still may make sense if you think there is an appreciation side to the story.

3. Return on Cash: My personal favorite metric of the three is return on cash. Basically, "I had some cash I wanted to invest. I bought an asset. How much money is that asset making me?" What I love about this metric is that it is so readily comparable to everything in the world around us. What's the S&P's annual return? What's your savings account earning you? What's a T-bill yielding? What's gold and silver done? What's oil doing? These comparables are everywhere to benchmark your performance against in mere seconds, and the comparables don't even have to be related to real estate in any way, shape or form. I just took a minute and searched for the 10-year return on an S&P ETF I own a few shares of and saw the 10-year average annualized return is 13.33%. This tells me something – If I think I can continue to get this same rate of return from this ETF, and I'm thinking about buying a vacation rental, I'd better get at least that amount from the vacation rental or I'd be better to just put the money into the ETF. Of course, you may not believe the stock market will continue to rise, you may want to diversify your holdings or you may want to actually be able to use the property as your own vacation place (in which case, return on cash isn't your only consideration). These are all things to be considered, and the ultimate decision is up to you. For me, I like to see 15% return on cash. 20% is great. 10% is not bad. You can also adjust this by putting more or less money into the transaction. For example, if the property can seller finance for 3% down, you'll have so little cash into the property that you're practically guaranteed a high return on cash.

Play with Your Budget – And Stress Test It

Excel is such a quick way to manipulate numbers that you can very easily run multiple scenarios for your property, and it's highly recommended to do so for a variety of reasons.

First, you can tweak the percentage of down payment and mortgage term to see how you will finance the property. Changing the down payment and term can quickly show different cash outlay scenarios and the associated income, payback and return on cash for each. Investing more cash into the property or increasing the mortgage term will lower mortgage payments, making the investment easier to cash flow and produce income, but it will also result in a lower return on cash and a longer payback period. Your goal is to figure out what fits your needs and wants for that property. For example, if you're looking to generate as much income as possible during your future retirement in 15 years, examine the situation where you finance every penny you can into 15-year loans. Can you live with the results? Or are you sitting on a large nest egg now and have the cash to spare, but want a stable, predictably-performing investment? Pay for the property in cash and enjoy the monthly return coming from it each month. How you proceed is often debated endlessly by various professionals, but what's important is that you're happy with the results. The Excel template can help you predict them.

When you've settled on some initial numbers for a down payment, furnishing and financing, what comes next is to stress test your scenario. Running three revenue scenarios at a minimum is recommended to test the ability of your property to cash flow under your *most likely* scenario, your *best-case* scenario and your *worst-case* scenario.

The *most likely* scenario is exactly what it sounds like – your absolute best guess at a realistic figure for expenses, occupancy rates and nightly rental rate. This is what you'll get most of the time, assuming your estimates are sound.

For the *best-case* scenario, lay out what could happen if all the stars align – a longer season, a lower repair rate, higher occupancy during the season, etc. Dream big. If you're normally a very financially conservative person, this task is harder. In a highly seasonal market, you may see best-case conditions for your peak month each year. Enjoy that month!

For the *worst-case* scenario, consider the looming disaster you hope never happens (poor occupancy, lousy weather, low rental rates and unexpected repairs) and see if you can weather the storm. We typically see these months when we decide to use a property for a longer portion of a month – since that essentially takes occupancy to a fraction of its normal amount.

Finally, some people like to consider a zero-income situation to see what happens if the property can't be rented for some reason and all expenses must be paid out of pocket. There's really no reason not to run these numbers given how quick and easy it is to compute in Excel, but there is limited true value to doing this because in the case of a major catastrophe that makes your property unrentable to guests, it's likely your insurance policy will kick in and pay for lost rent. You did get that coverage, didn't you?

Keep in mind that if things start sliding to the worst-case scenario in the real world, and you're predicting touch times of negative cashflow, there are always preventive steps you can take to minimize expenses. Refinance that 15-year loan into a smaller 30-year loan. Cut cable. Put in a smart thermostat and disable heat and A/C between guests. Delay some repairs. Short-fund your accruals. There are always steps you can take to mitigate losses if you're prepared for them.

In closing, remember that your budget is your plan. But it's not your bible. Execute to it as best as you can, but don't ever be afraid to rewrite the plan.

Chapter 3: Building a Network of Resources

On-Site or Remote?

Most people find a property they like, purchase it and then find a team to help them execute on their rental. It's easy to stay in a rental you love and see another unit in the complex on the market, and feel a strong desire to purchase it. After all, if the place you rented is cash flowing for its owner, why can't the one next door cash flow for you? While there is nothing fundamentally wrong with this approach, it's strongly advised that you find a general location you like first, then find a team to help you execute your vacation rental business and *then* find the property. If you think of your rental like a traditional manufacturing business, then this is like roughly defining what types of goods you will manufacture first, then finding a good raw materials supplier, a strong sales team and a reliable engineer before you begin to build product inventory. Just like this manufacturing business, you'll need people "in the office," which can be anywhere you're located to help you with the back-end work of receiving and issuing payments and handing contracts. You'll also need "boots on the ground" to handle cleanings, maintenance and other issues that arise in the actual property itself.

If your vacation rental is located nearby, and if you're quite handy, you may only need a cleaner. You may be able to get by doing the rest of the work yourself. This is quite a good approach and can really help your bottom line. But for most of us, you'll want to recruit some professional help. If your vacation rental is out of state, you'll need to recruit some help that you trust. But you won't need a huge network of resources. A cleaner, a handyman and maybe a local emergency contact you can count on if and when they're needed is generally sufficient. These resources should always be located close to your property because they'll be at your rental frequently.

Other resources may include a co-host you can rely on so you're not inundated with work managing your rentals completely by yourself, a marketing team and a pricing team. These individuals can be located anywhere in the world as they don't need to actually be at your property to complete their tasks. It's also not necessary to have dedicated individuals for these tasks. You can certainly do it yourself, but having these resources can make your life a whole lot easier and possibly make your property more financially productive. These resources do not need to be complicated or expensive to use either. In the case of a pricing team, for example, there are plenty of online services you can use that will optimize your listing's price for a small (typically 1% of gross revenue) fee; as long as they're improving your revenue, it's money well spent by you. For a backup or co-host, consider a friend, adult child or other trustworthy family member.

For *any* resources you choose to rely on for your rental business, it's always recommended to have the information for an alternative option on hand. Do your research up front just in case you need a contingency plan – always have another option at the ready in case your usual cleaner or handyman is unable to do the job. Often, this can happen with little warning because they are sick or have a family emergency. Other times, you may have some warning because they have a planned vacation or other event. In any case, having a backup can be the difference between giving your guests a seamless experience and a nightmare at check-in.

Marketing Resources

Airbnb, Vrbo, HomeAway and other popular sites do a great job getting your property listing in front of potential renters. They become your all-star sales team, building large lists of potential renters and showing off your listing to them. Except in very extreme cases (such as if you will only offer monthly rentals), you won't need any other sales resources. These sites, especially when used together, are quite enough to fill a vacation rental to its potential capacity because the list of people shopping on these sites for vacation home rentals is enormous. Five to ten years ago that wasn't at all the case. But today, Airbnb alone has over 150 *million* users.

Although the popular vacation rental sites do a great job at helping you *sell* your property, they don't provide you anything but a blank canvas on which to *market* it and make a potential guest want to rent *your* specific property. Sales and marketing must go hand in hand to have a successful business. The difference is just the same as in traditional business; sales without marketing may land you a few customers, and vice versa, but when the two work together to make a product people want to buy, then put it in front of people to enable and persuade them to buy, the results grow exponentially.

The difference between sales and marketing is subtle yet important. Picture a door-to-door salesman that rings your doorbell to sell widgets. Let's even pretend you really, really want to buy some widgets so you don't chase him away. You invite him in, and he shows you hundreds of widgets, all in-stock and ready to deliver today. That's his job – showing you widgets in stock and processing the order so you can get whatever widgets you want. Because there's hundreds to choose from, this salesman is not qualified to tell you why one is better than the other; it's just too much inventory for him to be trained on the details. He can sort blue from red, big from small and inexpensive from expensive, but that's about it. He helps you eliminate widgets that don't meet your needs, but he does nothing to help you choose the one that best meets your needs from the final candidates. When you've narrowed down your selection to a few widgets that may work for you, you have to rely on the widget manufacturer's marketing material to make your final decision. In other words, the marketing material is what's going to actually close the deal. The marketing material does not need to upsell you from small to big, or inexpensive to expensive (you've already filtered these out anyways); it simply needs to inform you about why a given widget is the best widget of its type. This is very different than traditional sales where the salesman closes the deal. In online marketing, you close the deal sitting behind your computer, on your own schedule.

This widget example is the exact methodology used when booking a vacation rental. If you've ever stayed in one yourself (and if you haven't, you really should before buying one!), then you've likely gone through a very similar shopping process on Airbnb, Vrbo or HomeAway. You enter the zip code and some dates (your initial filter) and a ton of homes pop up – probably dozens of pages worth of homes. How do you sort through all of these? You may filter on three bedrooms, two or more bathrooms, a pool and a hot tub, and find maybe 10 to 20 properties remaining. You may tweak the price dials a bit to filter out the few expensive outliers you can't afford, and find 10 homes remain. You'll likely look at each of these and check the reviews. Since they're all priced similarly, you'll ditch the ones with 3 stars or less in favor of the higher-ranked properties. From there, you'll open the remaining few and see what catches your eye until you've been wowed by either the pictures or the description (marketing collateral) of one. And that's your rental!

As the property owner, your goal is to own and manage the property that people are compelled to book when they finally open the detail page. If you're the first property people want to book, several great things can happen. First, you can command a higher nightly rental rate. Second, you'll keep higher occupancy rates. Third, as you do more of #1 and #2, you'll rise to the top of the search rankings, making it even easier to keep your property full at premium rates. This is called organic search engine optimization (SEO), and it leads to a great flywheel effect. But it can only happen with great, well-aimed marketing. *Chapter 7* delves deeper into how to boost your SEO.

Hopefully we've shown you why effective marketing is extremely important, but don't worry, creating strong marketing content can be a bit tricky, but not overly difficult. Your marketing team may be just you, or you may hire the help of a property management company, a freelance designer, a photographer, a copywriter, a videographer or other similar resources to take your marketing collateral to the next level. For your first rental, it is highly recommended that, if you don't have any photography skills (and that means access to a digital SLR camera, not your iPhone), then you should you hire a professional photographer. Similarly, if you're not a great writer, you should find someone with experience to help you write your listing details. These two marketing efforts are the most important; the rest of the marketing efforts can wait until you have enough profitability to support them. Most online sites aren't using videos today anyways, so video can be your last effort when you start to grow your sales channels outside of Vrbo and Airbnb.

Hiring a professional photographer can be a great way to differentiate your listings from most other properties. The very first Airbnb I stayed in used (as their cover shot) a giant "YIELD" sign outside the front door of their home. No joke. The picture was supposed to be wowing me with the picturesque mountain view from their home, but the YIELD was in focus and the background blurry. They could have walked two feet past the sign to take the picture to make it 1,000 times better. So why did I choose it? Unsurprisingly, it was the cheapest thing on Airbnb at the time and it fit my budget. As it turned out, it was a wonderful property, but a professional photographer would have more than paid for themselves by enabling these owners to earn a significantly higher rental rate and close more bookings.

If you're mildly skilled with an SLR camera, by all means take your own photos. There are countless books dedicated to the topic of real estate photography, and we've even included a short chapter in this book to help you take your amateur photos to the next level. If you're not skilled with an SLR, no worries, just leave the job to someone that is!

The same recommendation applies to copywriting. Finding a talented copywriter is very easy, and in today's online world you can hire experienced copywriters very inexpensively. Upwork, Freelancer, Fiverr and other similar sites all feature talented writers that can help. But unlike a photographer, they'll never see your property in person. Get your photos taken first and send them to your copywriter. Better yet, write your own copy first, focusing strictly on the facts you need included, then let the professional writer add the flair that makes it sing. Dollar for dollar, this may be the best investment you'll make in your entire vacation rental business.

Co-Hosts & Other Resources

Co-hosts are a wonderful addition to your team, and we recommend everyone have one (or more). A co-host may work full time with you and fill a gap you aren't as skilled at (for example, if you're shy in talking to your guests, let the co-host handle the communication while you focus on pricing and coordinating cleanings). This arrangement can let you focus on your strengths and the aspects of your rental business that you enjoy, while freeing you from the parts you don't enjoy. It can also allow you to have considerably more free time. Managing your property can be time consuming, and if you ever want to get away from it for a few days, having a co-host can be a very easy way to escape without adding stress.

Your full-time co-host may be as simple as a spouse, adult child or friend, or it could be a hired professional. Whoever you use, they don't need to be expensive, but they should be reliable. Your co-host will likely be part-time or on-demand; the benefit here is that if you are paying for their services, you can only pay as-needed. Life is unpredictable, and there will be a day when you need to step away from your rental. Having someone you trust to step in and take care of it on your behalf can be the difference between a smooth transition and a looming disaster.

Even if you regularly have immediate family that serves as a co-host, we recommend you have a backup outside of the family so you can escape your rental business as a family. For our personal situation, my wife is the first-line backup for when I'm traveling on business, and a good friend (who also hosts her home and thus is very familiar with the platforms) is our backup for when we are both unavailable (such as during our vacation time or family emergencies). Your family vacation will be much more enjoyable (or your emergency a tad less stressful) knowing your rental is in competent hands. Put this person in place well before a major vacation and have them manage the property for a period of time while you're fully available so that you can supervise them to make sure they don't have any questions or issues. They should learn your business when you're around to help, not by trial-by-fire. It's a bonus if they actually visit your property because then they'll be familiar with it when a guest asks questions, but you can also provide them tons of photos to acquaint them with the details they need. And we mean tons – take a picture inside every kitchen cabinet, kitchen drawer and linen closet so your co-host has the resources available to use when you are off-grid. Also make an index of where each item in your property is located. Your co-host will appreciate it, you'll appreciate knowing they have it, and if your guest asks a question, the guest will appreciate that you've made it quick and painless for them to get an answer.

One final note about co-hosts and our preference to keep things simple for our guests: Airbnb and some other sites allow you to designate a co-host that can message your guests from their own account so your guests know exactly who they're chatting with. Our personal preference for the ease of our guests is to never use this feature when working with a co-host. We only work with people we trust implicitly, and because of this we just give our co-host our login information so they can chat with our guests as if they are us. Our guests never know if they're talking to us or the co-hosts. In fact, our Airbnb account is in my name and my name solely. Even when my wife messages our guests, she messages them as if she is me. Anecdotally, it was a little weird at first when I looked back through the message history with a guest and saw my name signed to notes I didn't send, but I quickly got used to it. So far, only once did I read a message supposedly sent by me that referred to "my husband." While this method is our preference, it's not necessarily a recommendation. Giving out your password should not be taken lightly, so you can make your own decision of how to best balance your security with your guest's convenience.

Cleaning Services

Of all the resources you'll employ, your cleaner may be the most valuable to you and your business. Your cleaner is the primary touchpoint your guests will rate you on; more reviews, both positive and negative, will be about the cleanliness of your property compared to anything else. Get a string of good reviews on your property's cleanliness, and business may take off. Get a string of poor reviews, and you'll plummet to 3-star territory and no bookings quickly. Always hire the best cleaner you can afford, and always take good care of them. They are arguably the most important component of your business and should be treated as such. Know their birthdays, make notes of their children's names and always give them a holiday bonus. The right cleaner will be well worth this investment on your part.

You can use a professional service or, in major vacation rental areas, you'll likely be able to find an individual or very small business (perhaps a family) to work with. Either can be successful, but the one-on-one service provided by a local cleaner may offer you some advantages, even if the costs are higher. The local cleaner will have a reputation to keep that an individual employee of a large company may not. With a small family business, the family will likely handle the work personally, or at least ensure the same cleaner cleans the same property every time. This setup ensures the cleaner becomes familiar with your property, which is essential for making sure items don't go missing and for spotting any damages.

In a well-priced market, you will be able to pass 100% of your cleaning costs on to your rental guests, so don't be afraid to hire a good cleaner. Depending on the arrangement you have with your cleaner, you may want to charge your guests a little more in order to retain some of the cleaning fees for yourself for occasional recurring services like window cleaning, carpet shampooing, grout cleaning and other a la carte deep cleaning services. Your cleaner may also provide these services for you as needed for no additional cost, provided you use them exclusively for your cleanings. In either case, the result is the same: your rental guests should pay to keep your space clean, not you.

If you plan to clean your own rental, it's often tempting to charge a significantly lower rate for cleaning than competitive professionally-cleaned vacation rental units because it's all "profit" for you, and low cleaning fees can be a way to set your property apart from the local competition. This may work, but employ the strategy very carefully. We generally don't recommend you proceed this way unless there is a very compelling reason to do so. We've found this method is often not the best choice for several reasons. First and foremost is the value of your time; professional cleaners charge the rates they do because it takes time to do the job right. Assuming you also plan to do the job right (which you should), then you should be charging to cover your time and equipment in a similar fashion. Second, if you are fortunate to live local enough and have the flexibility to clean your own rental, this can be a great source of additional profit for you. Don't give it away just because you can; this is one area your budget can really shine because you have an advantage most people don't have. Don't be afraid to make some money! Third, situations change. You may grow tired of cleaning your own rental or you may move further away or take a new job that prevents you from doing it. If you're relying on any repeat business, now you will find yourself in a situation where you need to explain to your repeat guest why the prior year's $30 cleaning fee is now $85. It is better to avoid this situation from the start and price your cleaning correctly regardless of who performs the service.

Handyman Services

A good handyman (or woman) is crucial to keeping your property looking and functioning as it should. Having functional mechanicals, clean paint and everything operating smoothly is a major factor in earning positive feedback from your guests.

You will never get a pass for missing a cleaning. If your guest checks in to a dirty place, your review will suffer. With handyman services, a guest is more apt to understand that issues do occur. After all, you can't predict when an A/C capacitor will fail, a hot water heater will leak or a doorknob will loosen. But what you can control is how you respond to the situation and how much impact the issue has on your guests. A handyman that is on the scene lightning quick can salvage your guest's experience. In some cases, we have even seen this enhance it by earning the host a "super responsive" rating in addressing the issue.

The key points to a good handyman are both responsiveness and ability. They should be familiar enough with your property to know what they may need to service it, they should be on site quickly and they should get any issues fixed the first time as best as possible.

Key questions to ask your handyman include:

• What licenses or certifications do you hold?

• What is your average response time?

• Do you work off-hours (emergency response) and, if so, what is the fee?

• What services can you perform (e.g., electrical, HVAC, plumbing, etc.)?

• What is your rate?

• Do you offer preventive maintenance? (It may be cheaper to have your handyman do this rather than hiring an HVAC technician for preventative maintenance, but not all handyman services will service every appliance.)

You as the owner should have at least a vague idea of permit requirements for repair work. Your handyman should be closely familiar with it. Remember, you're running a legit business, so pull your permits.

We recommend you work closely with your handyman to determine potential failure points that could lead to a difficult guest experience, and plan ahead for them. If your handyman doesn't stock the parts you may need to get you out of a bind, you should consider stocking them yourself. As a personal note, we stock quite a few items. We've found the total dollar value of stocking one each of the below items is often less than the emergency replacement cost of just *one* of these items from a dedicated electrical, plumbing or HVAC company. For us, it's also just peace of mind. Items to consider stocking (should your property require them) include:

- Basic toilet/sink repair parts – gaskets and seals

- Fuses (not common in newer properties)

- Water heater anode (depending on your water conditions and heater style)

- Contactors for refrigerator and A/C

- A/C start/run capacitor

- Batteries for any oddball items you may have (CR2032 or coin cells especially)

- Smoke detector batteries (better yet, just put these on a preventive maintenance schedule or get 10-year batteries on day one)

- Furnace filters

- If your windows or doors require any service parts, consider these

- Evaporator pads for humidifiers

- Basic internet/cable cheat sheet for your handyman (if your internet goes out, your handyman is likely your first point of service to try to troubleshoot – make them a cheat sheet!)

- Spare keys – for the property, the laundry room, the garage, the mailbox, the boat, the snowmobile and whatever else you may have that your guests have access to. It is not recommended to give your guests direct access to the *spare* keys (hence the reason you should keep them with a handyman). If a guest loses a primary key, the handyman can copy the spare and then replace the primary with the copy. Also, should something need service and your guest have the key and not be home, the handyman can use his own key to complete the work.

- If your handyman is licensed to complete work on A/C units and your unit uses the older style R-22 refrigerant, it is nice to know that your handyman has access to this, as the refrigerant is no longer produced. This is not required (most handymen won't stock it, and you'll have to call a dedicated HVAC company). It is also not recommended you stock this yourself. But if your handyman stocks it or has good access it to R-22, it may be the difference between him/her completing emergency HVAC work versus you requiring an emergency HVAC technician at a significantly higher fee.

- Any other items your specific property or accessories may require. We won't delve into an exhaustive list because this varies by property, but for example if your lake house comes with a boat, stock a few maintenance items for it.

The key takeaway here is to prepare for the most expected and most likely problems that will arise because you'll be ready to handle them when they happen without breaking the bank. Don't put yourself into the spare parts business though. If you have more than a few hundred dollars invested into these items in total, you've stocked too much.

Professional Property Management

Finally, some owners do end up using professional property management services – sometimes to supplement their own work and sometimes to take a total hands-off approach to their property. If you want to own a vacation rental because you want to use it for part of the year, but your schedule doesn't allow you to do much of the hands-on work yourself, a professional property manager may be just the ticket. But the fees can be quite steep!

In some cases, the property manager will provide turnkey services. They'll take over the entire property, tweak the furnishings, take the photos, list the property on a few sites, handle bookings, meet and greet guests, handle payments, take their cut and send you a check for the profits and a 1099 for the taxes. In an arrangement like this, you can expect an average fee of 20% to 25% of your rental revenue after cleaning fees as the cost. You can build this into the budgets provided in this book to determine the effects on profitability should you choose to go this route.

In some cases, the professional manager may have a specialty that fills a gap that you're unwilling or unable to fill yourself. For example, they may manage the front-end (listing the property, confirming bookings and messaging guests to confirm) but then leave the cleanings and physical property management to you. In other cases, it's the opposite; you can list the property and confirm all bookings, and just send your property manager a list of dates the property is occupied, and the manager will make sure cleanings are scheduled and executed and the property is ready for guests. They'll likely also coordinate any maintenance or repairs needed and check over the property when a guest checks out. In either of these two arrangements, you can expect to pay around 10%, depending on your local market conditions.

Bottom line, regardless of what tasks you're trying to get off your own plate, there's likely a service that already exists to make it happen if you do some searching. Keep in mind that these services will eat into your bottom line, however. Make sure the cost is worth the time savings to you and that you're getting your money's worth from your service provider. It's recommended to never sign a very long-term contract unless you have a good escape clause.

Chapter 4: Getting Rental Ready

Choosing a Target Demographic

The first step to getting rental ready is to determine who you would like to rent to, as this will affect numerous other factors down the road. Of course, with vacation rentals you don't get to choose your ideal customer every time, but you can certainly tailor your property's amenities to suit the needs of a key demographic. You can set your pricing to attract a specific income segment, and you can furnish to draw a certain crowd (for example, to draw families you may provide bunk-beds and board games in one of the bedrooms).

Choosing your demographic is entirely up to you, but your location and property type will certainly have a major impact. If you're in Orlando near Disney, for example, you'd better be kid-friendly if you want to maximize profit. Arizona? Consider retirees. Colorado? Cater to the outdoor enthusiast, and so on. Spend some time in the general area of your vacation rental if you aren't already familiar with it and see who frequents it. Do you see younger or older people? Families or couples? One couple or two or more traveling together? Whatever you see the most of is likely your target demographic, but you can always force-adjust this if the market will bear it.

You can choose your target demographic in multiple ways, including:

Age: If you plan to cater to younger millennials, these individuals are likely more tech-savvy than most boomers, so offering the latest home automation, simple electronic self-check in, and furnishings that cater to a younger crowd is appropriate. If you want to target retirees, minimize the tech, keep the cable TV and furnish with items more appropriate to this demographic – perhaps a more classic decorating scheme and fewer contemporary items.

Couples vs. Families: If you're catering towards couples, you don't need to worry about any child-friendly features in your vacation rental, but if you're catering towards families, it's always nice to add in some touches that help parents deal with the young ones. For example, consider purchasing a high-chair, a bathtub instead of a walk-in shower, some extra cleaning supplies to make it easy for parents to clean up any messes their children make, and perhaps even some games for kids (maybe a video game system to help keep kids occupied).

Activities: In some markets, you'll have a chance to choose a demographic based on activities. For example, you can cater to the avid hiker and mountain biker, or the vacationer that prefers laid back jeep tours, hot air balloons rides, beach-days or just staying in. In the case of the former, perhaps you'll stock a backpack they can use for dayhikes, a cooler they can keep in their car while they're out hiking and maybe a small bike toolkit or floor pump. In the case of the latter, maybe you'll double-down on the TV entertainment options, add local brochures for tour companies and add more board games, spa towels, etc.

When you've figured out what demographic you will cater to (or where the bulk of your revenue will come from), take the time to develop a firm understanding of the preferences of this

50

demographic. For example, families want ways to entertain the kids, have access to more flexible sleeping arrangements (to separate kids), multiple TVs with smart connectivity so they can hook up their existing devices to the TVs, and board games and other activities to keep the children occupied should the weather turn ugly. Millennials on the other hand may prefer smart tech, a well-stocked kitchen and trendy furnishings. If you're marketing towards retirees, avoid too much smart technology – keep it simple! If in doubt, find people you know that fit this demographic and ask them. Better yet, let them tour your property if possible and give their feedback. This is especially important if you are not a part of the demographic you are aiming at, since your needs will be different. Even if you are part of your target demographic, however, your opinions may not match everyone in that group, so getting advice from others is always helpful as you begin to furnish your property.

Furnishing: Where to Spend and Where to Skimp

As discussed above, you should already have a core demographic in mind, which should help guide you in your furnishing style. For example, if you are catering to a younger crowd, always include electronic charging pads and USB outlets in each room and consider entertainment options like Smart TVs or YouTube TV, while if you're appealing to retirees keep the technology options basic, like an easy-to-use TV with basic cable. Whether the majority of your guests are high income, low-income, or somewhere in between, aim to make them feel at home with your furnishings. Each demographic group will prefer a particular furnishing style that you need to take into account.

While you should keep your key demographic in mind, it's important to still keep your property generally appealing to a wider audience as well. Generic artwork, a common color scheme throughout the entire property, a generally decluttered space and tasteful and highly useful furnishings will help keep your occupancy levels at optimum levels. As you do your competitive research of other people's property listings, you'll probably notice that the same artwork pops up time and time again. There's a reason for this: affordable and tasteful artwork that is well suited for a particular part of the country will be in high demand. Other vacation rental owners in your area went through the same furnishing process, and it's a great idea to let their choices inform you of what style you should select for your property. If you find a particularly great example of a competitive Airbnb doing something you absolutely love, don't be afraid to mimic it.

Unless you really want to cater to the ultra-luxe vacation rental experience for your guests, the general recommendation is to furnish in a mainstream and affordable fashion, spending your money where it maximizes the guest's experience or promotes an asset's longevity. Especially with the more expensive items, such as couches and dining table sets, it is worth the extra cost for durability, but not for couture. Hopefully you'll have many, many guests using those furnishings, and you don't want to have to replace them every six months or have negative reviews concerning the worn and stained furnishings. You'll have to decide that delicate balance between if it's worth it to pay more for the more durable item, of if you're better to buy cheap and replace more often. Depending on the exact item (and oftentimes the simplicity of replacement) the answer may vary. When purchasing towels and sheets, for example, always buy cheap and replace often. For couches, chairs, appliances and other semi-durable goods, however, you may want to consider spending more up front for higher durability.

The living room will generally take the most abuse, and a sturdy but simple coffee table that can be sanded down and refinished after taking a year or two of abuse may be a wise investment (provided you can do this work yourself). It's important to keep the furnishings useful for your guests as well; always make sure they have a place to set down a glass from any chair, stool or couch in the room. If a coaster is always within reach, it's likely to get used, and you'll benefit from that. A pull-out or sleeper sofa is also a versatile option that is useful for guests not wanting to share a bed, especially when separating children. It goes without saying that you should install a TV in the living room. Smart TVs are a must today, but choose your connectivity options based on your demographic. Sometimes a simple Netflix account is enough, or consider Roku, Apple TV or a Fire stick so guests can log into their own accounts. If you are aiming for retirees, we've found many still prefer cable TV as opposed to a bring-your-own account option.

If you have a dedicated dining room, make the space as usable as possible; a table that can be expanded is always a plus, even if the room is a tad tight when the table is at its maximum length. If you don't have the space for a full dining room, a small breakfast table that seats two or stools along a kitchen island can be a nice option for your guests.

Each bedroom should have a smart TV either mounted to the wall or sitting atop a bureau across from the bed. If it is a bedroom meant for adults, a nightstand on each side of the bed is essential so the guests have a place to leave a glass of water and charge their phones. Queen size mattresses seem to be the norm these days, unless you cater to a more luxe group that prefers king. If you have a room geared towards children, bunk beds are a space efficient option. For any beds, make sure the mattresses are comfortable and the bedding is soft and plentiful – but it's not recommended to spend for luxury in this area. Instead, replace often. You'll also want to stock extras of all sheets, pillows and blankets. An iron and ironing board, luggage rack and plenty of hangers are also basic requirements. It's very important to remember that you are offering people a home, not just a place to crash for a night. The more your place feels like home, the happier your guests will be, the better it will be treated by your guests and the better you'll do in your reviews.

If you plan to offer the use of a kitchen as a selling advantage, go all-in. Don't have the bare minimum in your kitchen because it might be the difference between your guests being able to cook their meal (thereby earning you a positive review) or not (leaving you with a negative review about the kitchen you oversold). Not everybody will use your kitchen, but in our experience those that do will have a *very* strong voice about it being functional. Don't be afraid to spend some money here. That doesn't mean top of the line, but it does mean completeness. A five-piece mid-range cookware set is better than a two-piece top of the line set, and a full assortment of bowls and plates for 12 people from your local Target or IKEA store is far better than a high-end selection of plates for four. If your property is equipped with a dishwasher, make sure all of your dishes, utensils and other cookware are dishwasher safe. You won't have to worry about anything being destroyed when a guest accidentally runs your nice carbon steel knife through the dishwasher.

The only area you should never, ever skimp is safety. Make sure you have up-to-date smoke detectors in each bedroom, hallway, basement and elsewhere as required by code; carbon monoxide alarms in each bedroom and near combustion sources (get the 10-year battery versions so you don't have to worry about changing batteries every six months); fire extinguishers (with the locations noted in your welcome book); non-slip shower mats; outlet covers (if you cater to young children); de-icing salt (in winter climates); secure locks; pool safety items and any other safety items that your property requires. Spending here isn't optional; these are necessities, and a penny of prevention is worth a dollar of cure.

The details of your furnishings will vary a bit for various demographics, but there are a few recommendations that apply universally:

- Furnish the walls with nice art, trying to be reflective of the local area as best as possible to help your guests feel immersed in the locale. In the desert? Hang cacti pictures. In the Pacific Northwest? Oceans or mountains should work best. But don't overdo it; not every wall needs 10 cacti! Keep it tasteful and decluttered.

- Furniture should always be comfortable, but keep in mind that rental furniture has a short shelf-life compared to anything you've had in your private home. You will probably replace it every five to seven years, so aim for cheap but nice. Skip any costly add-ons like stain protection; you can do this yourself with a can of spray protector. Whenever possible, it's recommended that sofas be sleepers so you can accommodate extra guests or separate children or friends. It makes your space more flexible, unless of course your strategy includes not catering to families with small children.

- Furniture should also look coordinated rather than ad-hoc. It's always okay and even recommended to look at used furniture; it can be a great way to minimize costs and boost return on cash, but don't furnish randomly. The property should look well put together, and the items in each room should coordinate.

- Identify items that are nearly disposable and spend the least money here. Glasses break, silverware gets lost or destroyed, plates chip, towels stain, sheets rip and so on. We always recommend buying twice what the property needs and storing half, because when this happens you have an immediate replacement on hand and don't have to worry about your pattern or color no longer being available.

- Linens should be comfortable, including towels, but per the above also keep these cheap. Yes, cheap but good exists. Buy in bulk. A diaper pad used by our first guests in one of our rental properties destroyed our sheets when they forgot to remove it and washed it. I didn't care one bit because we buy sheets 12 sets at a time for about $3 each; we tossed it into the trash and moved on. Make sure what you buy is comfortable, but don't overspend.

- Buy large towels. Your cleaners may hate you (because they take longer to dry), but your guests will love them. Stock plenty, but keep them cheap (hint: Amazon Basics work great). We also recommend keep all linens white. They can be bleached, they don't fade and they don't react with any skin-care products that can have a color-lightening effect. If you have a pool, it's also a good idea to provide beach towels to save your shower towels from getting used outside. Sometimes, we also stock black microfiber towels as well that guests can use for anything from cleaning their shoes to cleaning their bikes or cars after a long day in the mud.

Simplify Your Workflow with Technology

Technology is wonderful when it works but can kill your rental business when it doesn't. Whether you choose to employ technology to simplify your life or improve your guests' experience, keep it simple. Very simple. If you're not around to manage the property and your co-host is covering for you, they'll need to be able to operate whatever systems you have put in place as well, so make sure your systems are within their abilities to troubleshoot and repair.

If the technology is connected to a touch-point for your guest, aim for simplicity. Any guest, from the tech-savvy to the technophobe, should be able to operate everything in your property without instructions. If it takes instructions to work, it's too complex. Your renters are there to enjoy their time, not spend it trying to power on a complex stereo/TV/receiver. Of course, even with the most basic system, you will still receive occasional questions from guests, but keeping things intuitive will improve your guests' experience and keep you from being their IT helpdesk.

You'll also want to stick with tried and true products that have strong histories of performance in a rental environment. We do not advocate any particular brands, but below are some touchpoint items we suggest you consider in your rental:

• Smart lock. A smart lock, which can be operated and programmed remotely through an application, is the best piece of tech you can own, for yourself and for your guests. It simplifies the check-in experience, eliminates the need for your guests to carry (and possibly lose) keys, lets you "change the locks" between renters with a few button presses, and lets you monitor who (including your cleaner and handyman) is coming and going. It also offers great peace of mind when you can check and confirm that your cleaner has arrived before a same-day turn. Smart locks have revolutionized the vacation rental business for owners and guests alike, but they can fail. *Always* install a backup lockbox for these occasions. At all costs, avoid the few brands in the market still hanging to a "Paid Virtual Key" model that charges a fee to create multiple door codes. Opt for one that lets you program codes on the fly for no additional fee.

• Smart thermostat. A smart thermostat allows you to program and remotely control the HVAC for your guests. While it is not a critical feature, a smart thermostat can save you significant money in the long term, since you can limit how much a guest can adjust the thermostat (want to set A/C to 62? Not in our rental!). You can also fully disable the climate system remotely when vacant, and monitor the status including when it's time to change filters or perform service. Finally, most smart thermostats set a time limit. If a guest does make an adjustment, it can be set to revert back to a more energy efficient temperature in a few hours.

• Internet connected TV. Whether you prefer Roku, Chromecast or any other smart TV, the trend is clear that most renters, especially those with kids, want to hook up their own devices to your TV. Gone are the days when cable is mandatory, which can also amount to a large savings for you. Just toss a few smart TVs up on the wall, connect them to the internet, and your guests will generally figure out the rest these days.

- Motion lights. Outdoors, motion lights can be great for your guests. When they arrive and park, they'll be greeted with plenty of light to ease their entry into your property.

- Smart lights. Sometimes your property just isn't laid out the way you or your guests prefer, and light switches can be in unusual locations. Smart lights and smart switches can be added virtually anywhere to simplify turning lights on and off, but keep it simple. If you're using these to build complex setups, you're using them incorrectly for a rental property. *Keep it easy.* And no voice controls.

- Video doorbells. Never put a camera inside your rental, even if you make your guests aware of it and tell them how to disable it when they arrive. Every guest will be uncomfortable with it (and rightly so). But a well-placed doorbell camera outside can be a great tool for you to monitor who's coming and going, and for your guests to reach you immediately with the press of a button if there's a problem. This can also help you detect when extra guests that haven't paid are arriving, or when the cleaners are coming or going (so you know the property is ready to go).

- Miscellaneous. There's a ton of tech out there, and a variety of unique situations that call for a specific application to make life easier for you or your guests. Employ technology as you see fit, but always remember that good tech should integrate seamlessly. It should simplify the guest experience, not be a source of annoyance. It should fit smoothly into your and your guest's workflows by speeding up check-in or check-out or improving their overall stay. If you can't train your co-host how to manage it in a few minutes, it's not the right tech, and your guests won't have the patience for it.

Creating a Welcome Guide

The welcome guide is your guest's bible upon arrival. Many guests don't do much up-front planning for their trips and rely on these guides religiously to plan each day on-the-fly. Other guests may book up-front the one or two special things they want to do in your area and plan the rest of their time with suggestions from your guide. We routinely hear from our guests that they actually use the suggestions we make in our guides. The time and effort you put into your guide will pay you back a healthy return in terms of happy guests and positive reviews. Also remember that your guide should be dynamic. Keep it updated with information of new restaurants, stores or activities in the area. There's nothing worse than that wonderful restaurant you recommended to your guests that closed a month ago.

Always make a printed version of your guide. It's very professional for your guests to walk in and see the home guide printed and waiting for them. You can also consider a digital version; if a guest is asking for recommendations for the area, you can simply email them the guide. They'll appreciate having it in advance (but this is not a substitute for having it printed in the property). Having a digital version ready to send also eases the burden for you to provide personalized responses to each of your guests; simply send the guide and be done.

The guide should generally contain the following topics, but you can and should customize it to the needs of your location or property:

- House rules, especially check-in and check-out instructions, quiet hours and any other pertinent property-related information

- HOA or association rules

- Other relevant local ordinances

- Safety information such as escape routes, locations of fire extinguishers how to dial 911 (which foreign visitors may not know) and the location of the nearest hospital. Also list the property's address and any relevant information that someone could relay to 911. Remember, many of your guests won't *really* know the details of where they are staying. Google got them there, and in emergencies, people don't think straight. Make it easy for them.

- Internet username and password

- Instructions for operating anything unique to your property (such as a complex coffee maker)

- Map of your property, especially if it's a larger multi-unit complex or has amenities scattered around it, like pools or tennis courts

- Area map. Highlight the key attractions.

- Detailed list and description of local attractions. It's desirable to segment this into categories based on the various types of guests you expect. For example, "Child Friendly Attractions" could be a category, or in an area known for outdoor activity, "Easy/Moderate/Difficult" could be helpful sub-categories to include. Categories based on activity type is another common example, such as "Golf/Hiking/Biking/Beaches"

- List of items in the condo and where to find them. Ideas include laundry supplies, soap, extra linens, pillows, board games, wireless router, kitchen appliances, coffee pot, etc. If in doubt, list it. This is like your index of possessions. Keep it easy to navigate (alphabetic or grouped by room).

- List of local restaurants. You may want to personalize the list with your favorites, and many guests will appreciate a tip on pricing. This can be handled by just writing a one-sentence description for each with "Affordable Casual" or "Elegant Upscale" or other similar language to describe what the expected price point might be.

We also recommend you supplement your house guide with plenty of books on the area. Many guests will appreciate these, especially if they end up staying on a rainy day and just want something to read. It also lets your guests know you're thinking about their needs, which will be reflected in their reviews of your property. Simply stocking a copy of a travel guide goes a long way. Look for niche books as well, such as "Visiting Southern California with Kids" or similar titles to let your demographic know you're attentive to their situation. I always also try to leave a few books on local history, flora and fauna, buildings or other topics a bored guest may want to check out on a rainy day. Finally, it's fun to leave a pen and ask your guests to make their own recommendations in these books or in your guidebooks. This way, your guests can help you improve the recommendations you make for future guests.

Chapter 5: Photography Tips to Make Your Listing Pop

Written by Julie Mencel – Owner of Pro Copy & Design, a full-service photography and marketing company.

DIY or Pro?

Your property pictures should always look professional, but you may be able to take them yourself if you are equipped with some basic photography equipment and a little skill and patience. I'm not talking about using an iPhone; you need a decent digital SLR camera and access to Photoshop or other similar editing tool. While I will make specific reference to Photoshop Elements, the most common tool in the hands of a hobbyist photographer, there are a number of editing solutions to choose from, both paid and free. If your goal is to maintain maximum occupancy in your properties, it is important to treat it like a business. What you don't know how to do yourself, hire out! But never be afraid to try or learn new things. With photos, there is no harm in trying yourself first and outsourcing later if you're not happy with the results. But, if you have little to no photographic experience or equipment, you may find that your time is not worth the effort to acquire gear or learn the art for only a single property. In this case, hire it out, write the check and spend your time focusing on the things you excel at. I'll assume you have decided to handle the photography on your own (otherwise this chapter would be quite short), and I will cover some basic equipment, staging, composure, lighting and editing techniques. This is far from a comprehensive review of real estate photography, since each of these topics has been the subject of many books. The goal here is simply to provide you with a few tips and techniques to make your photos look professional and appealing.

To adequately photograph your property, you'll need the following equipment:

• Digital SLR camera

• Minimum of one (two preferred) flash units. For smaller properties, the on-board flash might be sufficient to light your property if you use a few creative tricks I'll delve into later, but nothing beats the power of a dedicated flash.

• Photoshop Elements or CC, or other similar photo editing program

• Wide-angle lens (especially useful for smaller properties)

• Normal lens (around 50mm). Most likely, the lens that came with your camera covers this range.

• A tripod may be helpful in composing a shot but is not required provided you use flash – no need to worry about motion blur in these shots.

Staging the Space

The property should look clean, and less is more in most cases. Remove any personal effects, do a general decluttering and set the stage as though you are preparing the property for a very special guest. This might mean staging a nice bottle of wine, some fresh cut flowers, a nice bag of local coffee next to the coffee pot and all the little touches that you would not necessarily provide for a standard guest. It goes without saying that the property should be clean, but take extra care to vacuum the rugs and couches, detail the grout lines and really make it in A+ shape. It should be the best that property will ever look. I generally even try to ensure the carpet knap lies flat and consistent and the couch fibers are looking uniform. The better you can make the property look upfront, the less time you will have to spend in Photoshop later.

Shooting

I always take a variety of shots; you can then appeal to a variety of guests and you will have more to work with later in postprocessing. Some shots are rather straightforward, non-artistic shots designed to showcase a specific portion of the property such as a newly remodeled shower, and some shots are designed to create a little more emotion behind them. These photos give your guests the information they need, while leaving a little bit of intrigue to see the rest. Since only by booking can they actually see the rest, this increases the likelihood of someone choosing your place for their stay.

I always shoot in RAW so I can tweak light balance later, but many people have perfect success with JPG, so this is a bit of preference. I spend the most time on the cover shot, which is the first photo you'll list on the vacation rental website. I try to always show the living room in this shot (unless there's some other amazing feature of the house that makes it unique – for example if photographing a unique dome house, I would show the dome in the cover shot). If you can also include a kitchen in the cover shot along with the living room, that's a huge plus. If your floor plan doesn't allow it, focus on the living room. 90% of the time, I shoot with a wide-angle lens to show as much as I can in the cover shot. The larger your space looks, the better. I used to find this practice a little deceptive, preferring to show properties using only a normal (50mm) lens, but unfortunately it is now standard in the vacation rental market to photograph with a wide-angle lens. Thankfully it seems as though most potential renters are well aware of this practice, and it has become more accepted. Very few people these days will balk at a host using an ultra-wide lens.

For the cover shot, I try to shoot one that will evoke some emotion. Point-of-view shots work great here. Can you fit behind the couch to shoot over the back of the couch, where a guest would sit, aiming at the TV they might watch? Or looking out the gorgeous windows with mountain views? Shoot a little lower than you would normally, crouch a bit for a unique perspective or shoot diagonal across the space. But always remember to hold the camera very level, as any perspective distortion will quickly reveal you are using a wide-angle lens. But if you need to shoot off-level due to limits in composition, don't worry too much; you can fix much of that later in Photoshop.

Figure 1: Left: This shot was taken with the camera just a bit higher than a human head would be on the couch. It feels uncomfortable. Right: Lowering the camera just a few inches changes the feel of the entire space and makes the viewer feel as if they're seated on the couch.

Next, I try for a few close-up shots in the living room such as the couch with the nice mural behind it or the recliner facing the TV. This lets the viewer focus on what is important to enjoying their stay. Next, I move to the kitchen. I always try to show an overview of the kitchen, assuming the room looks nice, and to stage a few selective small appliances such as the blender, coffee maker or the teapot, just to show they exist. These are purely informational shots, with no emotion. As long as it doesn't look cluttered, feel free to show off what you have to offer your guests. Sometimes, if the home has a unique cooking feature, like an outdoor grill, I'll also include that in the kitchen section.

Figure 2: This is an example of what not to do. The angle feels awkward, the wide-angle lens actually makes it feel smaller, and there is a major flash hit on the cabinet to the left of the microwave, combined with underexposure underneath the cabinets. Don't do this!

Figure 3: Recomposing the scene a little bit really helps with the feel of the image, but the front-facing flash has left flash hits on the front counter and microwave, and large ugly shadows behind all of the appliances. Yuck! We'll discuss how to fix this shortly.

Figure 4: Finally, pulling back just a touch shows even more of the space, and the flash is corrected to point up, illuminating from the ceiling. The window (exterior) is properly exposed, and there are no major flash hits. The reflections on the windows, stainless appliances and granite counters can be cleaned up in Photoshop if desired, but otherwise, this one's ready for your listing!

For the bedrooms, I prefer one straight on-shot of the bed and nightstands, one straight-on shot with a normal lens showing the amenities on the night-stand with part of the bed, and two oblique shots, one from each side of the room, typically also with a wide-angle lens. These latter two just aim to show the décor and any bedroom amenities.

Figure 5: This nightstand shot shows a clean setup that a guest can expect: an alarm clock, table lamp and wireless charging pad. It's a nice, clean shot that conveys good information without distraction.

Figure 6: Pulling the camera back a little bit and shooting wide angle from the foot of the bed can give the viewer an "imagine yourself here" feeling. This image was shot handheld and is a little bit off-level (notice the bottom of the closet door curving inwards). A 10-second touch up in Photoshop can take care of that! When you're working on location, don't sweat the small stuff if it's an easy fix later.

I don't take many pictures of the bathroom unless it offers something unique to set it apart from other properties (such as a jacuzzi or a fresh remodel). Sometimes these small spaces do not photograph well, and in these cases you may only want one informational photograph included in your listing. Pay attention to mirrors; they are very challenging to photograph and will wreak havoc with your lighting and post-processing work. Also, always check you aren't reflected in any mirrors!

For the exterior, I shoot two series of photos. The first is a very simple walk up to the property, starting from the street and showing what a guest driving to the property would see. These are simple photos with no artistic touch and will be used for the check-in instructions later. I always use a normal lens for these. Show the view from the street, the view from the driveway and, using approximately six shots, walk the guest to the front door and into the property (show the house number location, the keypad and door lock/lockbox). Remember, by the time the guest sees these, they've already booked. The goal here is simply to provide clear information to your guest so they can locate the property and settle in as quickly and seamlessly as possible (and to reduce the likelihood that YOU get a phone call from them).

The second photoshoot of the exterior is to cover your amenities such as a pool, basketball court, lake, boat or snowmobile. With these amenities, I try to build a little emotion without making them overly artistic. It is okay to be creative, as these amenities differentiate you from your competition. These amenities provide the icing on the cake. When possible, I try to show these amenities in-use. Showing a boat sitting on a trailer in the yard is much less appealing than showing a picture of the boat in the foreground and a child waterskiing behind the boat in the background. Stage these as best as you can, but make them realistic. Don't show waterskiing if your property is on a no-wake lake. Choose fishing instead, and catch the moment you reel in a keeper! Finally, when shooting the home's exterior for the marketing shots, I try to remove any identifying information about the property, since these images are being shown to the world. While it's no problem to show this information to a paying guest, for general security reasons I don't disclose any identifying information about a property before the guest books. The exception here may be if you're in a multi-unit complex and your individual unit can't be identified from the photos.

Lighting

Lighting is another topic that can easily be an entire book to itself. But for our purposes, we will keep it very simple. After all, the goal is for you to get better pictures of your rental, not to deep dive into the Nikon Creative Lighting System.

I like to photograph most properties with the window treatments open (assuming there is a nice view), but this can take a lot of light from a flash to overpower the sunlight outside. If you have access to an external flash, use it. Point your flash straight up or just slightly tilted forward, and shoot with the flash in automatic mode. Never point your flash directly forward; you'll get hotspots and shadows. If you are using the built-in flash on your camera, tape a folded up white business card to the front of the flash to direct the light upwards. Don't use your hand or a colored card, or you'll discolor your image. Trust me: you will never go back to a flash-forward picture again after trying this lighting tip. But with the built-in flash, take care to check the exposure of you picture. The small flash may not have the power to expose your photo properly when using the business card trick, and if you are fighting bright sunlight, you just may not be able to pull this off. In that case, wait until it is a little darker and try again. The reduced sunlight outside will give your small flash a fighting chance. Closing the shades is another option.

Figure 7: Attaching a simple folded white business card in front of your flash to direct light up to the ceiling can improve photos significantly - just make sure your flash has enough power to light your scene, or you'll end up underexposed!

When shooting with open window treatments, I always set the camera to Manual mode, expose for the windows, and then let the flash do the heavy lifting for the inside. The result is a beautiful and well-lit scene straight out of the camera with little Photoshop work needed. Just make sure you aren't getting flash reflections on the window glass; if you are, move your lighting, camera or both until you are happy with the results. If you know how to use your flash wirelessly, this is an ideal method. This can be the fastest path to eliminate reflections, assuming you don't want to change your composition.

Figure 8: Left: A no-flash shot with properly exposed outdoors (left), leaving the kitchen nearly black. Center: Still no flash, this shot exposes for the kitchen but blows out the highlights from outside and leaves the countertop with strong reflections. Right: Same exposure as the left panel, but adding indirect flash to light the indoors.

Lighting for outdoor shots is simpler. If you are shooting an object, then I try to shoot on a bright overcast day to minimize shadows. I like to use a little fill-in flash to bring some dimension, shooting usually straight-on flash with -1.0 to -1.3 flash exposure compensation. Note, this is the only time I will shoot with the flash pointing straight forward, but I can usually get away with it because the flash is not the main light, it is just lifting the shadows a bit. Just watch the flash reflections on shiny objects like a waxed boat. You may also find moving the flash off-camera helps. If you can't move it off-camera, just eliminate the flash hits as best as you can and use Photoshop to fix the rest.

Editing

Specific edits for each individual picture vary depending on lighting, composition, subject, etc., so my aim is to give you a few simple fixes to the most common issues you will experience in real estate photography. Instructions are written for Photoshop Elements 2019, which is the program used by most amateur photographers. Editing steps are very similar for Photoshop CC.

First, consider the photo shown below. While it is not a bad shot, the lighting is a little dark. My favorite method is to adjust the Brightness up and the midtone contrast to make it pop. It gives it an HDR-like quality, and the viewer can really see details. In the toolbar, click *Enhance > Adjust Lighting > Shadows/Highlights*. From here, make subtle adjustments to each of the sliders until you are happy with the result. *Lighten Shadows* and *Darken Highlights* both compress the brightness range. This can be very useful when dealing with areas of bright light (sun) mixed with areas of shadow. Midtone contrast can be boosted afterwards to eliminate the dullness to the photo often seen after the previous two adjustments are finalized.

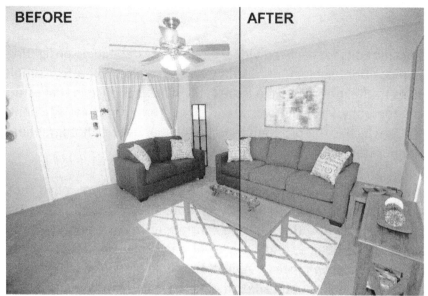

Figure 9: Left: This shot is a bit underexposed, showing the grey couches as black and leaving the floor looking dingy. Right: Proper exposure and a boost in midtone contrast brought out the best. The floor and furniture look great! Ignore the wide-angle distortion for now - we'll fix that later.

Perspective distortion, especially when caused by a wide-angle lens, can be difficult to fix perfectly in Photoshop and is best handled as much as possible in-camera. But due to composure, layout and other factors, it is not always possible to get the perfect composition in-camera. When you can't do it in camera, Photoshop's Perspective Distortion tool can be used to improve the look of your photo. Compare *Figure 9* to *Figure 10*. *Figure 9* (especially the door and TV stand) are at awkward angles and far from the vertical they would appear in real life. The walls are no longer falling backwards in *Figure 10*, and it has the appearance of being taken with a normal (50mm) lens, except for the slight vertical compression. I handle this using *Image > Transform > Distort*, because then I can adjust the four corners individually. For an easier fix, use *Image > Transform > Perspective*. They work similarly, but Perspective keeps the picture symmetric as you make changes, whereas the Distort feature allows asymmetric changes.

Drag the corners in or out until your picture looks more natural. Don't overdo it; depending on the lens you used and the angle you shot at, you may have to find a tradeoff between vertical lines and overall vertical compression. A full-frame 12mm lens shot off-level will generally produce an unnatural looking image, even after extensive Photoshop work. If you can't get it to where you are happy, first reshoot closer to level in-camera, then come back to Photoshop.

Figure 10: The image above has been corrected to eliminate as much perspective distortion as possible. The overall image is better, but the space looks a little short. Further cleanup to stretch the image vertically could help.

There are a few more tools you can try on your own that are particularly useful in real estate photography. The first two are the Spot Healing Brush and Clone Stamp. If the floor is dirty but you don't have a vacuum on hand, you can use these tools to clean up the shot. They can achieve similar end effects, but depending on the nature of your photo, one may be faster, easier or more effective than the other.

The next tools I'll leave for your experimentation are the Sharpness and Blur tools. Often, pictures right out of an SLR (especially those shot in RAW) lack sharpness, and a quick touch up can lead to a much better overall photo. Try *Enhance > Auto Sharpen* or for more control, try *Enhance > Adjust Sharpness.* Sometimes you want to make a little blur. When we photographed our first rental, we hung the curtains up and forgot to iron them before we photographed the place and left town. When we got home (a few states away), we saw the pictures and saw how awful the curtains looked. We used Gaussian Blur to soften the creases (*Filter > Blur > Gaussian Blur).* In this case, we had to first select only the curtains, so we used the magic wand tool to highlight the curtains, then right clicked and selected *Feather* to soften the transition area for the blur effect (for feathering, try different amounts – the size of your image and the size of the area you have selected will affect it). The result is that the blur fades nicely into the sharp areas and looks natural. You can also try the Spot Healing Brush first before applying the blur if more effect is needed.

Enhanced Marketing

Years of marketing various businesses' products on Amazon has taught me much about how people shop and make buying decisions, and the rules I've learned from creating enhanced lifestyle photos on Amazon apply equally well to Airbnb, Vrbo, HomeAway and other vacation rental sites.

Lifestyle images are images that showcase a product in use or in its intended application. They invoke an emotion that the consumer can relate to and help create the feeling of an experience the viewer wants to share. For a vacation rental, this generally means showing images of what your guest could be doing in the home or local area. Building on the above example of the boat, you certainly could show a picture of a boat on a trailer, or better, a boat in the water. These are descriptive photos, but not very emotional. A lifestyle image may show someone waterskiing behind that same boat, carving into the wake and smiling. You don't just want to ride on that boat, you want to be having the same amount of fun as that person. Marketing is most effective when it shows what *could be* to the potential guest.

Similarly, if your area has lakes, show people swimming in them. Show people on hiking trails, on horseback, lounging on the beach, climbing a mountain, touring a museum, exploring the city's bridges or similarly enjoying whatever your main local attractions are. You can take these pictures yourself, or you can purchase stock photography.

I also prefer to overlay text onto the lifestyle pictures in addition to the standard image captions. These text overlays should be short but can be quite effective. When implemented effectively, they can strongly reinforce the lifestyle image. Also, on vacation rental sites, very few people tend to use overlay text, making them a simple tool that will set your listing apart from the competition. Below (*Figure 11*) is one example of a lifestyle image we have used in a listing.

Figure 11: An enhanced image with a text overlay can be a great way to grab your potential guest's attention.

Chapter 6: Creating & Maintaining Your Listing

Scoping out the Competition

Before building your listing, do a thorough competitive survey. Take a look at other listings in your area. What appeals to you? What doesn't? Look at photos and read text copy. You'll likely see a variety of styles in the listings. Some are very casual and easygoing, while others are stern and businesslike in tone. You'll see well written and not so well written copy. You'll see friendly tones and less friendly tones (the latter is especially prevalent in the house rules section). Where do you want to position yourself in the mix? You'll have to decide your comfort zone between being too stern that no one wants to book, and being so overly easy-going that either your guests complain when you try to enforce the house rules or you just attract the wrong types of guests because they think they can do whatever they want. You need to appear business-like yet friendly.

How you sound to your potential guests is what marketers call your *tonality*, and it helps your guest understand what to expect from you – a clean, professional experience like staying at a JW Marriott, or a fun, laid back experience like staying at a Sandals resort. Both of these options are very different, but equally acceptable, provided the experience matches the needs of your target demographic. You'll need to choose where you want to fit in, but in general even if you will be on the serious end of the spectrum, it's highly recommended to not take an overly stern tone in your listing. You can both keep it serious and keep it light.

As you read competitive listings, try to decide what type of person the listing is targeting. Young couples? Families? Business travelers? Retirees? As the demographic changes, how does the tonality change? Pay particular attention to the things you don't like and the reasons you wouldn't book a particular listing. What about it makes you not want to book? Is it too loosely written to the point you can't understand what you're actually getting? Is it too sternly written to the point you're worried your host won't let you have any fun? Make a list of the things you don't like so you can reference it later.

Next, pay attention to the things you do like. Even listings you don't like will have appealing elements to them, so be careful not to dismiss an entire listing as one you wouldn't book. Rather, read it thoroughly to understand what you do like about it.

Finally, if each listing you read is a pixel, the totality of listings in your area should assemble together into a clear picture of your vacation rental market. Do you see any gaps of property types or listing styles that are missing? Try to analyze why these gaps exist. If nobody is marketing to families with small children, this just might be a good niche you can target. But if nobody else is doing it, first make sure there's not a good reason for that. Perhaps most travelers to the area don't have small children, so if you stock your rental with cribs and baby toys, you may end up with too small of a market to succeed.

Writing Compelling Marketing Copy

Once you've determined what tone you'd like to employ, it's time to start building your listing, beginning with writing the marketing copy that helps your place get booked. Marketing copy is the text that makes up your property's name, description and additional information you provide about your property and your general location. The marketing copy should be accurate and descriptive of your space. Of course, it's a marketing piece, so a little creative license is warranted. The goal is to paint a description of how your space outshines the other vacation rentals (but never use direct comparisons). You want to let your guests know what to expect when they arrive but also paint the picture of the lifestyle your guest can experience if they stay in your property.

Strong marketing copy draws you in from the first sentence and makes you want to read more. Unlike the house rules (discussed below), which should be very concise, bulleted and specific, the marketing copy can be drawn out (but not to the point of rambling). Often, vacation rental websites will put strict word limits into their forms, so you'll have to find a good balance between providing enough information in a concise manner and providing enough detail about the space to draw the potential guest to your property and make them want to book.

Consider the two descriptions below. In a moment we'll analyze what makes each effective or not.

Home #1:
Title: Kalispell Condominium near Glacier National Park
Description: This condo is located in downtown Kalispell, MT. It's 5 miles from the entrance to Glacier National Park and is well-stocked with amenities such as a full kitchen, two bathrooms, and four bedrooms with queen beds (sleeps 8 total). You can walk to restaurants and nightlife. There are also books and brochures on the area and a wood fireplace and memory foam mattresses.

Home #2:

Title: Glacier National Park Getaway

Description: Nestled in the heart of Glacier National Park, just steps from the main entrance, this charming condo is a great respite after a hard day of hiking, horseback riding or adventuring. With sleeping for up to 8 people, you can bring the entire family or your best friends to experience the magic of the park with you! The condo is stocked with guidebooks, maps and brochures to help you plan your perfect Glacier adventure. The full kitchen lets you enjoy your own cooking, or if you'd rather spend your evenings relaxing, the location in downtown Kalispell is within walking distance of great restaurants and nightlife. Or, grab some takeout, head back and light a fire in the natural wood fireplace before retiring to the comfortable queen-size memory foam beds.

Where would you be more likely to book? Home #1's description was short and very factual. In fact, both descriptions contain the same *factual* information. However, Home #2 paints a picture of what a typical day might include, and how that specific condo can be a piece of that day. It appeals to a potential guest's emotions and also focuses on a specific demographic of hikers and adventurers. Home #1 doesn't make any attempt to create a feeling for the guest of what their day might be like; it merely informs them of what to expect when they check into the condo. Home #1's description isn't *bad*, it's just not nearly as appealing as it could be.

What's most important is that neither description lies, misleads or misconstrues information. As a host, you should *never* do this. Set a very clear expectation of what your guests can expect at check-in, and they'll never be disappointed. The best compliment I can get from a guest is "The place is exactly as described!" This lets me know my description is accurate, and while you may want your guest to find some nice surprises when they arrive, if you're going to spend the money on these nice touches, you should flaunt them in the description to help you improve your occupancy rate or to be able to secure a slightly higher nightly price. In fact, when I see a review stating "I was pleasantly surprised that..." it's a red flag to me that I need to go back and add that feature to the listing description. Always remember: the goal of the listing description isn't to secure you 5-star reviews, it's to secure *bookings*. Bookings equate to revenue, so do what you can to secure as many as you can. It's the property and your hosting style that secure you the 5-star review. All are important, but the description should focus solely on getting bookings.

When writing your copy, consider both what makes your place unique and the reasons why people come to your area. Perhaps you have similar tastes as the typical guest and are quite familiar with the *main* reason people come to your area, but what do people different than you like? Perhaps you love hiking and laugh at the people in the Jeep tours – or vice versa. Remember, those people comprise half of your demographic, so be sure to appeal to them as well. If an area is particularly known for one feature or activity, such as the beach, mountains, hiking or mountain biking, then feel free to market that area or activity heavily. If the area is known for many activities, you can highlight a few mainstream ones, and, like in the description for Home #2 above, use general descriptors like "adventuring," "relaxing," "exploring" and so on to appeal to a larger audience and avoid pigeonholing your listing.

If you live in a tighter market, either one that experiences a down season and you want to maximize your bookings in this period, or a market that is just flooded with an oversupply of vacation rental properties, it's even more important to appeal to a wider demographic to ensure your property is booked as much as possible. Keep your ideal target demographic in mind and focus the copy to be directed to this group, while being inclusive of others as well. A rookie mistake we made early on was to intentionally not market towards families in an attempt to limit small children in our first vacation rental, which we assumed would reduce wear and tear. It quickly became apparent that our off-season bookings in the summer months dropped noticeably because that time of year is popular with families on summer vacation. We rewrote our description to appeal to families and saw a boost in our occupancy rates shortly thereafter. In fact, the property never even saw excess wear and tear from children! We were wrong on two counts, but quick action on our part turned the situation around quickly. Lesson learned!

Finally, most vacation rental websites have a maximum word count you can use for each text field, and we recommend filling that space as best as you can. The more descriptive your listing is, the better. But take care to eliminate all unnecessary words; emotional, compelling copy is great, but filler is not. Consider the following, adapted from Home #2 above:

Option 1:
This condo is nestled in the heart of Glacier National Park in Montana and located just moments away from the park's main entrance. This charming condo is a great place to call home after a hard day of hiking, horseback riding or whatever adventures you may experience here.

Option 2:
Nestled in the heart of Glacier National Park, just moments away from the main entrance, this charming condo is a great respite after a hard day of hiking, horseback riding or adventuring.

Both Option 1 and Option 2 contain similar descriptors, but Option 2 trims a few non-critical filler words to form a more concise, engaging sentence. When character count is capped, it also gives more room for the text that matters. As William Zinsser states in *The Classic Guide to Writing Nonfiction*, "Examine every word you put on paper. You'll find a surprising number that don't serve any purpose." This style of writing takes practice, but you can read your sentences carefully, selectively removing a word or two each time you read it to see how it affects the delivery of the message. Remember, your writing should be engaging and draw the reader in; make it too long and the reader will give up partway through, taking their booking elsewhere.

Writing Effective House Rules

Compelling marketing copy grabs a potential guest's eye and makes them want to take a closer look at your property; when they do, the house rules is often their next stop. House rules define the host/guest relationship and set clear expectations for both parties. You'll want to put some controls on your guests' behavior, and your guests will want a clear understanding up front of what's required from their end if they book.

Effective house rules should be friendly in tone, yet firm in delivery. You want to give your guest a perfectly clear expectation, free from ambiguity so they know what is and isn't acceptable. It is important to deliver the message in a friendly tone.

Consider these three brief listings of house rules. Which would you rather stay in? Which do you feel is too ambiguous?

Home #1:

- *No partying.*

- *Quiet hours are strictly enforced from 10pm – 7am.*

- *Do not park in any spaces other than the two assigned spots.*

- *Do not bring any additional guests without permission or you will be charged $15 per person.*

- *You must empty all trash when you leave.*

- *No pets or you will be asked to leave.*

Home #2:

- *For the enjoyment of all guests on this property, we ask you respect quiet hours from 10pm – 7am.*

- *Please park in the two spaces reserved just for you, right in front of the condo, #5 and #6.*

- *If you decide to add additional guests, please modify your reservation on Airbnb to add the additional guests so we can keep an accurate count of who's coming. Please note, we have a maximum of 6, and guests over 4 incur a $15/person/day extra guest fee.*

- *When you check out, please take any trash to the dumpster – it's conveniently located close by your two parking spots. All other items can be left as-is for the cleaner.*

- *Please note, we are unable to accommodate pets at this time, and will charge a $200 additional cleaning fee for any unauthorized pets.*

Home #3:

- *Please be quiet and respectful during evening hours so other guests on the property can enjoy their time too.*

- *Please park only in the assigned parking spaces.*

- *When you check out, please make sure the condo is left clean.*

- *Please no pets or a pet fee will apply.*

Looking at Home #1, the tone is overly and unnecessarily strict and aggressive. It may turn off some potential guests, making them think you are an overly strict host. It does, however, send a clear message to the guest on expectations. You will see many, many house rules posted like this on Airbnb and Vrbo. After one or two less than ideal guests, many hosts retaliate with overly strict house rules. It's an understandable reaction, but it's not good for your business.

Home #2 also send a clear message to your guest – but in a much friendlier tone. It defines the exact expectations for your guest and lets them know (in the case of extra guests or pets) the repercussions of not following the rules. It tells them the parking space numbers and sets a clear expectation for checkout of what's to be done.

Compare Home #2 to Home #3. In Home #3, the message is also fairly friendly, but very vague in its delivery. Depending on the property, this may or may not be okay. Consider the first bullet point regarding quiet hours. If you are in a condo complex with HOA-defined quiet hours, it's advisable to make your guests aware of the details to avoid a potential issue later. If you're in a single-family home with no nearby neighbors, it may be perfectly acceptable to avoid a defined quiet hours schedule; the choice ultimately needs to be yours based off your individual situation. It's always better to err on the side of too much information in your house rules rather than too little. You can think of your house rules as the contract between you and your guests. If you have an issue with a guest and need Airbnb, Vrbo, HomeAway or similar third party to mediate, your house rules will be one of the main platforms on which arbitration is made. After all, if the rules aren't well defined, you can't really fault a guest for breaking them. It's your responsibility, not your guests', to make sure the rules are understood by all.

What you put into your house rules is ultimately up to you, but some suggestions of areas to focus on include:

• Allowable check-in times. Is there a latest-possible check-in?

• HOA rules and regulations

• Quiet hours

• Parking

- Check-in procedures. Do you want your guests to contact you upon arrival, use a lock box, etc.

- Check-out procedures. Is there a cleaning regimen you want guests to follow? Where to leave the key? If you offer a parking pass or any other item normally left in a car, document a reminder here for your guest to return it. Detail the fee if they forget.

- Pet policy. Do you allow pets and, if not, what is the fee if they bring one?

- Number of guests. Are people outside the reservation list allowed in for visits? What is your fee for extra guests?

- Party or event policy

- Any additional fees related to lost keys, early check-in, late check-out, etc.

- Cancellation policy. Unless your vacation rental platform already has a built-in cancellation policy documented (Airbnb and Vrbo both do), explain your cancellation policy and any related fees.

- Any other relevant, property-specific rules you want your guests to be aware of.

Defining Your Booking Settings

The specific listing details you can control for your vacation rental vary a little bit from platform to platform, but all platforms let you control a basic set of features including how guests book (instant booking versus sending a booking request), available dates and pricing. Most platforms have some built-in tools to help you manage these settings, including discounting tools, automatic pricing (Airbnb calls it Smart Pricing) and calendar integrations so that you can link calendars from multiple sites together so dates blocked on one site are automatically blocked on other sites.

In addition, there are numerous third-party tools available to link multiple properties to a common dashboard, automate your pricing or handle your bookings for you. When you are just beginning, these tools can be nice to have, but do incur additional costs. Consider what you want to do yourself and what you're good at and/or enjoy, and then think about outsourcing the tasks that don't fit your strengths.

Pricing is a large topic, so we'll cover that separately in its own section. For other booking settings, the critical two to consider are how a guest can book and when a guest can book.

As far as how a guest can book, the decision is to allow automatic bookings, or for you to review each and every booking and confirm it. In general, it's recommended to always allow instant or automatic bookings. There is little to no real reason to ever require your guests to send you a request to book. Some hosts will argue they want to only accept guests with 5-star reviews or at least a few decent reviews, but in the end, the anonymity of these platforms means you really don't get to pick your guests anyways, so there is no point to try to control the uncontrollable. If you require every guest to send an inquiry before you authorize them to book, you'll miss out on many opportunities to gain bookings from guests that prefer the immediacy of instant book. We're all busy people; adding in a few extra steps and potentially a lot of extra time for both yourself and the guest will certainly limit the number of guests you'll book. Remember, always keep it simple for your guests!

The booking window, or the distance into the future you allow your guests to book, is another important consideration. If you frequently use the property for yourself and don't plan too far ahead, you may want to consider a short booking window for your guests. Hopefully this this isn't your case, however, because a longer availability window can lead to increased revenue if executed well. Even if you use a shorter booking window, you may want to open up some key dates based on certain holidays, long weekends and special events in your area to help drive some revenue.

You should know what your competition is doing already. Just scan the various rental sites. If you select a longer booking window than your competitors, you'll be one of only a few properties available way into the future, so you can potentially charge more per night for these bookings since availability is low. Of course, not many guests are searching for dates very far into the future, so this may not work if your competition is using six-month windows and you try for a 12-month window. But if your competition is using three-month windows and you try a six-month, it can pay off nicely because it's not so far into the future. This price skimming usually couples with the pricing strategy of lowering your prices as you get closer to the date. For example, if you typically charge $100 per night on average, you can try $125 four to six months out, then drop to $100 for bookings two to three months out. For reservations within a month, you may also then be able to drop below $100 per night and still maintain an average nightly rental rate equal to or greater than $100 since your distant bookings offset your immediate bookings. The result may be the average rental rate you want with a higher overall occupancy – win/win!

We briefly mentioned holidays and special events. You should be intimately familiar with all of the major events going on in your area and particularly which ones you can use as major revenue sources. Open these dates immediately and with a large price premium, especially for annually recurring events. Many people will book their stays for the following year while they are in town for the event. If you're one of the only available properties, guess who's going to get the booking?

Setting Your Pricing

Aside from availability, pricing is the most important factor for maximizing profit. If you can make your vacation rental command a higher nightly price (without changing expenses), you will make more money. In the real world, pricing is more complex and in most markets is highly intertwined with availability and expenses. As your price goes up, a few things happen:

1. Less people may be interested in booking, which means a smaller pool of people to draw from and potentially lower occupancy. In some markets, where demand is high and availability is low, this may not be an issue, but these markets also have a way of self-correcting over time; these markets tend to quickly get flooded with new vacation rentals as people try to capitalize on the high profitability.

2. As your pricing goes up, more will be expected of you as a host to continue to command such a high price, effectively raising your expenses. Or, more likely, the reason you are able to command a higher price is because you have a nicer property that is already more expensive. But remember, although a more expensive property will command a higher rental rate, the return on cash can be lower. This is not a hard and fast rule, and exceptions occur, but for the most part, the highest return on cash percentage is obtained from smaller, more affordable and modestly furnished properties, since these have the smallest cash outlay. Don't go seeking a property that can bear a higher rental rate if it ends up with a lower return on cash.

In general, a good pricing strategy means you charge the most that the market will bear for your property on that particular day of the week, time of the year and location. However, price isn't the only driver of revenue; occupancy is also important. Lowering your price can significantly boost occupancy, and sometimes it's desirable to charge less in order to make more revenue in the long term.

Consider two reservations on your calendar: a guest checks out on Tuesday, and another guest checks in Friday. You have three nights open in between these two reservations in a market where perhaps people typically book four or more nights; therefore, you have a pretty low likelihood of filling these dates. In such a case, dropping the price for these three open dates may encourage someone to book where you may otherwise have a vacant property. You're better to use an aggressively low nightly rental rate to secure a booking and fill the space. In practice, we personally get quite a few day-of reservations using this strategy, and for us it's worked quite well at making an average month into an above-average month.

Use caution with large price drops, however. You should always determine a minimum you're willing to charge, and never deviate from it. At some point, lowering your price may get you a lower quality guest or too little profit to make renting worthwhile. For each rental, you will have luggage wheeling in and out over your floors, washing of sheets and linens, new people in and out and general wear and tear. If you charge too little, you'll find it's not worth it to host a guest, or worse, you'll attract guests you may not want in your property at all. Some of our most difficult to handle guests have been booked at our lowest rates, and we've since made the decision for our own rentals to set a price floor that we never go below. Many of our headaches disappeared after this, and only a little bit of our revenue went with it. If you find you're frequently the lowest priced rental on Airbnb or Vrbo in your area, we recommend you take a hard look at your pricing and refine it upwards. If you find your rental doesn't do well when priced at *average* nightly prices for your market, you're likely doing something wrong elsewhere. Take a wholistic approach to solving the problem.

When you set your pricing, you can get creative and perhaps charge more for weekend nights, or offer shorter duration stays for a higher fee. For example, you can set base pricing for a four-night minimum, but then for a 10% extra fee allow shorter rentals down to one night. Not all platforms have built-in tools to handle these sorts of complexities, so you may get stuck using the inverse, which is a weekly discount. A weekly discount can be a nice way to secure longer-term bookings, but these may not always be the most profitable if you have to concede a lot in price to get them. Try to limit the discount you provide to be as small as the competitive landscape will allow. I also like to set a very low price for exactly one night each month, because when a guest finds your property without searching for specific dates, your lowest published price will be the one displayed on the page. Some may argue this is deceptive marketing because it draws someone in by showing a low price only to reveal later that most nights are twice the listed price, but the reality is that both Airbnb and Vrbo are set up to reward the hosts that do this. Even if you don't get any bookings from guests searching properties without specific dates, you'll help your search engine optimization and placement globally, meaning those guests that *are* searching specific dates are also more likely to see your property first.

Some sites also offer early-bird pricing for very distant reservations; this can be an interesting strategy, especially if you are holding pricing very high for these distant dates and then discounting from the higher level, since you don't really lose much anyways. Remember, your pricing should also be a moving target. Adjust it often to maintain a high occupancy rate. If you're using the early-bird strategy, you may find you need to discount as the dates get closer, so you have high nightly rentals with high early-bird discounts for the distant-term reservations, average nightly rates with no discounting in the mid-term and lower nightly rental rates in the very short term or in between other booked reservations. This can be a profitable strategy but will also require more of your time to implement effectively.

The beauty of short-term rentals is that you're never locked into a price level for long. As soon as your guests check out, you begin the process again with new guests and new pricing. The opportunities to experiment are huge, and the best hosts will use this to their advantage to experiment freely to figure out what works best. Draft up a few pricing strategies on paper and try each for a month to see what happens. You'll pretty quickly learn what works for your demographic and your location, and when you dial in to a method that works, stick with it. But remember, market conditions change, so check back in with your strategy often and adjust as needed. Sometimes, even tiny tweaks can help you fill your property much faster. You may not even always understand why a particular strategy is working, but just let your revenue numbers be your guide as you experiment. Always be careful to filter out normal seasonality effects from your pricing effects. If you're adjusting pricing at different times of the year, it may be hard to separate how much of your revenue change is due to seasonality and how much is due to the pricing strategy you've chosen.

When setting your pricing, don't be afraid to make money. We've worked with a few hosts that feel guilty when a guest pays a lot for their rental. We've actually seen people who think they're making too much profit, so they lower prices to make it more "fair" for their guests. Remember, you set your pricing and your guests willingly book – or don't. You're doing this to make money, so if the opportunity presents itself, make the money. Try for one month raising prices just $5 per night and see if your occupancy drops. If not, try to add another $5 the following month. Especially if you're a 5-star host, you may find you can go higher than you thought. You'll know from the occupancy percentages when you've gone too far, and then dial back to find the sweet spot where you're maximizing gross rental income.

Finally, if you don't want to actively manage your pricing yourself, many tools exist to do the management for you. But beware of conflicting interests built into these tools; many aim to get bookings at any cost rather than to maximize revenue. One such system is Airbnb's Smart Pricing. From our experience, we recommend avoiding Airbnb Smart Pricing and equivalent pricing algorithms from other platforms. These pricing algorithms are meant to adjust pricing automatically based on demand and some other factors, but really they try to maximize profit for the rental platform, not for the host. This typically means securing a large volume of bookings quickly, with less emphasis on the price each host receives. Remember, you're one of millions of properties to them, so if they make a dollar or two less in commission, they don't care. Frequently, the result is that price will be lowered automatically to secure a booking so they get their service fee, and the host is left with lower revenue on their one or two rental properties. Don't believe us? Turn on Airbnb Smart Pricing – then turn it off. It'll walk you through about four warning pages before it turns off, which is Airbnb's desperate attempt to scare you into keeping it on. Would they do this if it wasn't their cash cow? Trust me, set your own prices whenever possible, or use an independent third-party pricing management tool instead of Vrbo's or Airbnb's integrated tools.

Maintaining Your Listing

Listing your property is not a one-time event. Your listing needs to be maintained and continually improved until you've optimized it for your market. Even then, you'll likely continue to add amenities to your property that should be reflected in your listing description, or you'll make changes to your listing to keep current with the latest features Airbnb or Vrbo have added. Your listing should always be kept up to date in all aspects. If you're not using all of Airbnb's features, you're likely not going to get the best placement you can.

Review your house rules often as well. HOA rules change, you'll add new items or features to your property and you'll get feedback from your guests. The latter is of particular importance to address. You'll also get questions from potential guests such as "Is there laundry?" or "What activities are nearby?". As guests start to ask questions, consider updating your listing to address the most common questions you're asked. A well thought out one-time update to your listing may save you quite a few questions down the road, while simultaneously simplifying the experience for your guests and improving your occupancy percentages. Win-win.

One of the key drivers for optimizing organic search engine optimization, which is discussed in the next chapter, is frequent minor updates to your listings. The more time you actively spend on platforms such as Airbnb, HomeAway and Vrbo as a host, the more these platforms will reward you with better page placement.

Using Feedback to Improve

Guest feedback is always your #1 tool to improve. You should take all feedback seriously and adjust your property and policies as you are able to improve your guests' experience.

Feedback can take two forms: a direct line of communication from your guest to you during or after their stay or the more colloquial feedback where the guest writes a public review on the booking site (sometimes accompanied by additional private comments to you). Both are equally important and will help you improve your rental property – and therefore your rental income – over time.

When you receive direct feedback from a guest, especially during their stay, this is a great opportunity to show you are a responsive host. Their feedback may be positive or negative, but quick responses can go a long way. For example, a guest may comment "We love the coffee you provide" and you can simply write a response like "It's our favorite too – that's why we use this brand for our guests!". You've demonstrated that you are providing your guests with what you deem to be the best, and not simply what's cheap.

While situations like the above do happen from time to time, it's much more common that a guest's feedback will contain a complaint or suggestion for improvement. If the feedback occurs while the guest is still staying, and it's something you're willing or able to fix, it's always suggested to offer to fix it on the spot. For example, if a guest complains that a sink is leaky, a good response might be "Sorry to hear the sink isn't cooperating – would it be OK if I send a plumber to take a look? I don't want to disturb your vacation, so if you prefer, I can wait until you check out to address this." What you've done is shown responsiveness, shown that your goal is to minimize disturbance for the guest and shown that you care to remedy the situation in whatever way *they* deem best.

These responses go a long way. We had a situation where, shortly before their stay, a guest contacted us to ask if there was space in a bedroom for them to install an air mattress that they would bring. We immediately ordered the air mattress ourselves (thank you, Amazon Prime!) and told the guest that there was space and there would already be an air mattress waiting for them when they arrived. The guest was very happy and mentioned the interaction in their public review on Airbnb. For a small $50 investment, we made the guest very happy, improved our Airbnb rating and now have an extra feature (the air mattress) to offer future guests.

Unfortunately, many guests are hesitant to ask or complain about something during their stay but will do so in the written feedback on the booking site afterwards. This is always unfortunate when your guest doesn't give you an opportunity to correct something during their stay, but at least you can act on it for future guests. To help minimize the chances this happens, I usually check in with my guests at least once during their stay (unless the stay is only one night). Typically, a quick note via the booking app is all that's needed. My smart lock can tell me if they've checked in or not. I usually wait a few hours after they've checked in and send a quick message like "Just wanted to make sure you were able to check-in OK and that everything is to your liking?" I've found that, in doing so, I've minimized the chances a guest will post negative feedback without alerting me to an issue and giving me a chance to correct it first.

Depending on the platform on which you list your vacation rental, the feedback you receive may be public or private, and you can choose to respond or not. Private negative feedback should always be responded to – especially if public feedback hasn't been posted yet. If the negative feedback is private, respond also by private note with something similar to this: "Thank you for your note; we always take feedback very seriously. We've had a plumber come in to replace the sink hardware, so if you ever book with us again, rest assured it's handled!" This type of response is critical to send, because if you can get ahead of the public feedback, you may salvage it.

If negative feedback is public-facing, there are two schools of thought on responding. The first is that you should respond to *all* or at least *many* of your public reviews (both positive and negative) as a routine part of your business. This sets up a regular pattern of you replying so that any potential guests looking through your feedback don't immediately see the only response you've ever written is to negative feedback. Your responses to feedback, especially positive, can be very simple. "Glad you enjoyed your stay in our home!" is generally sufficient.

The second school of thought is that if you generally only receive 5-star feedback, don't worry at all about responding to positive reviews and respond to negative reviews only if extremely warranted. One negative review in a sea of 5-stars will quickly be overlooked by your guests. If the negative review is very specific in nature (e.g., the leaky sink), then by all means address it with a simple "Thanks for your feedback; the issue with the sink has been addressed". This lets future potential guests understand that you are responsive, and they will be more apt to dismiss the negative feedback. These kinds of negative feedback are very simple to handle with little emotion attached.

Responses to negative feedback when it lambasts the host or the property are much trickier to write. They often become emotional, so it's suggested to wait a day or two to respond if you're upset so that you can cool down before writing something you can't undo. First off, understand what the review is saying. Is the review mostly positive with only one or two minor complaints? Or is the entire review negative? Second, take a serious self-assessment. Are the points valid? Next, decide if you will reply at all. If the review seems to have the reviewer making an ass out of themselves and is the only negative review in your entire history, you may be better off to let it go. This is especially true if you have a series of new guests booked already, since their reviews will be bumped to the top, ahead of the negative feedback. If you decide to reply, focus on the real meaning of their feedback. If they are complaining about the leaking sink in the example above, their feedback might read as follows:

This place was falling apart, and the host wasn't responding to me. The sink was leaking everywhere and made a mess. The host didn't care at all, and the home is old and in disrepair. This should have been disclosed on the listing. Don't stay with this host, ever!!"

It's best to just address the root of the complaint (if you answer at all) with "Thanks for your feedback; the sink has been replaced." Keep it factual, non-emotional, and short.

It's important to note that you don't want to be seen as an overly emotional host. You want to be seen as a stable business that cares about its guests. However you respond, keep it simple, keep it short and keep emotion out of it. You'll host many, many vacation rental guests, so you *will* inevitably host someone you just don't like or you simply can't please. Let their time pass, let their review drop lower on the list and move on. It's miserable when it happens and it'll drive you a bit crazy, but remember that this is your business. You're trying to maximize profit over the long haul, so don't do something rash in the short term that jeopardizes your income.

Chapter 7: Marketing, SEO & and Growing Your Clientele

Organic Search Engine Optimization

If you've ever shopped at Amazon, you know that the most popular products in a category rise to the top of the page. In fact, there's a joke amongst many Amazon sales reps that the best place to hide a dead body is Page 2 of the Amazon search results. The majority of shoppers on Amazon never look past page 1 when making their purchase. For Airbnb, Vrbo, HomeAway and other similar sites, the same technology is working behind the scenes to bring the most popular homes to the top of the list, and the same effect is often observed. The homes towards the top of the list get booked the most. The best thing you can do for your property and your profit is to get your home to the top of the search results list. This will let you charge a higher price while maintaining higher occupancy, and therefore obtaining higher profit.

Unlike Amazon, most vacation rental sites don't have paid placement. You can't spend your money to have your place listed first. Instead, you have to rely on *organic* search engine optimization (SEO). This means that your rental platform decides to prioritize your home above others based on a variety of factors.

The criteria and methodology by which listings are evaluated is complex and generally proprietary, though Airbnb and Vrbo have commented on the factors that influence their SEO.

Key *direct* factors that influence your placement on most vacation rental sites include:

• The time a potential guest spends looking at your listing

• The time you spend maintaining your listing

• Your feedback rating

• Your overall number of bookings

• Availability

Key *indirect* factors that influence your placement include:

• Being a Superhost (Airbnb) or other similar advanced ranking

• Airbnb Plus or other similar advanced property designation

• Occupancy rates

• Pricing

The *direct* factors mean that each item has a direct and measurable impact on your SEO placement (although you may not be able to measure it, you'd better believe Airbnb and Vrbo can and do measure it). Most sites analyze the time a guest spends looking at your property. If they look for a minute and move on, you're ranked low. If they spend a lot of time reading the descriptions and rules and checking out the pictures, this will move you higher up in the rankings. It demonstrates you have captured someone's interest, even if they haven't booked. This is the reason longer descriptions are recommended. If you're given 1,000 words to use in a particular field on your listing, use them all. Add as many high-quality photos as possible. SEO is the most important reason why compelling copy and professional photos (and lots of them) matter. It'll keep you at the top of the results, which keeps guests finding your place quickly and booking it.

As mentioned in the last chapter, the time *you* as a host spend maintaining your listing is also counted by most rental platforms. They want to see that you're spending your time to make tweaks and changes to optimize your guests' experience. Log in often – daily. At a minimum, log in, update the price for one or two nights and then log out. These frequent touchpoints will keep you at the top of your potential guests' search results, and they're probably one of the easiest ways to help yourself stay current. Frequent small tweaks to your listing are generally better than sporadic major updates.

Feedback, occupancy and the number of bookings always factor into your SEO, and here the effect is more obvious. If you're a 5-star host, most platforms will favor your property over a 3-star or 4-star property. If you have a good reputation for taking great care of your guests, your rental platform will do what it can to keep a steady stream of them coming to you.

Finally, availability *seems* to play a role. The more days you block for personal use or because you've secured a booking from another platform, the lower you seem to drop in SEO. This is based solely on the author's experience and observations, but it seems to be a repeatable phenomenon. Each platform wants you to use their services; Airbnb doesn't make money when you close a deal on Vrbo. The more availability you offer Airbnb, the more exposure Airbnb seems to offer you. In general, it's best not to worry too much about this, because if you find your bookings are split across multiple sites about evenly, there's nothing you can do. But if your split happens to be something like 90% / 10%, you may want to ditch the platform providing the 10% and go all-in on the platform achieving the 90%. We've experimented with some properties in this manner ourselves and have been happy with the results, so it's a routine part of our own strategy now for certain locations.

Some factors don't directly affect your SEO placement, but rather have an *indirect* effect. They influence it in some way, shape or form. For example, many Airbnb users think obtaining Superhost status is the de-facto way to boost SEO. Airbnb publicly announced, however, that Superhost status has no direct effect. Rather, the steps you need to take to obtain Superhost status (positive feedback, a certain number of guests served or nights booked, etc.) are the real drivers. Superhost status in Airbnb does have a filter setting, so a guest searching for a property can choose to limit the results to only Superhosts, but that is the only direct effect of having Superhost status.

The keys to boosting SEO are persistence, patience and dedication. You can't push a new listing to the top of the list overnight; it takes time and good rental history. Do your part as a host to treat your guests properly; stay on top of your listing and pricing, and respond to your guests quickly, and eventually you'll reap the rewards. You're playing the long game here. But what you can do is try to pack a lot of guests into a short period of time by offering one- or two-night minimums. You'll get plenty of reviews more quickly by offering one-night minimums than you will by offering seven-night minimums, and you'll also have more touch-points with your guests, time spend logged into the platform and all the other factors that drive SEO.

Earning 5-Star Reviews

It's our opinion that the single best thing you can do to maximize your profitability is to earn 5-star reviews. This is true for many reasons. You boost SEO, making your listing the top of the search results and putting it in front of more people. You build credibility and instill trust with prospective guests, making them not only more likely to book, but more willing to pay than they would otherwise for a listing with fewer stars. You maintain Superhost or other similar status on your platform. You potentially attract the attention of Airbnb Plus or other advanced listing designations. All of these things boil down to maximizing your rental revenue.

We'll talk more about managing your guests in the next chapter, but we'll say here that the best things you can do to obtain 5-star reviews are twofold: 1) give your guests exactly the experience they expect – meaning clear, accurate descriptions in your listings with a friendly tone, so when they walk into the property, they have no surprises, and 2) help your guests out when they need it. This can mean being responsive. If someone asks where the laundry is, answer them immediately because they probably have dirty clothes in their hands already. Don't wait until you get home or after you finish the grocery shopping. Respond immediately; it just takes a minute usually. Helping your guests can also mean being proactive, such as taking a few minutes and checking in on your new guests after arrival. A quick message to make sure they checked in okay and found the place to their liking is all it takes, and that extra touchpoint can go a long way.

Also, consider offering value-added services. At the core, you're simply offering your guest use of a property in exchange for money, but if you can take this to the next level and also act as a small-scale concierge for them, you'll enhance their vacation experience and they'll likely reward you with glowing 5-star reviews about you as a host (not just about your property). These host reviews carry even more weight with potential renters looking at multiple places. A well rated host stands out from the crowd as a zero-risk option. Offer advice for your favorite hikes, tours, wineries, restaurants, museums and any other great local tips. Especially if they've never visited the area before, help your guests maximize their time and their vacation. Remember, for you it's just a business, but for them it's a vacation experience. Make it a positive memory for your guest and you'll reap the reward as much as your guest does.

As you gain some experience managing your rental, you'll get a feel for when you're likely to get a 5-star review and when you may get dinged on the review because of some factor either within or outside of your control. Almost like a sixth sense, you'll know when your guests are either overly difficult or simply not enjoying their time in your place. It's frustrating, but fortunately it's usually (but not always) salvageable. We'll dive deeper into managing difficult guests in the next chapter, but if you get the feeling you're heading for a less than 5-star review, be proactive. Reach out to your guest to see if there is something you can do to salvage the 5-star review, or at least secure a 4-star instead of a 3-star review. It's not always possible to save it, so if you can't make it work, don't sweat it. You'll get it back with the next guest.

Superhost Status

Superhost status on Airbnb (or its equivalent on other platforms) is generally the first aspiration of all new Airbnb hosts. You get a fancy badge, and you get your own "Superhost" tick box when people are searching for properties. Aside from that, there is actually little *direct* benefit to becoming a Superhost. Rather, it's the individual accomplishments (5-star reviews, having served a large number of guests, etc.) that collectively add up to Superhost status that offer you the greatest return. You should absolutely aim to be a Superhost, but don't consider it the game-changer that many people believe it to be. It's just a reflection of the things you've been doing right at every step along the way.

Where Superhost status may have an effect, however, is on your credibility, especially with newer guests. If a guest is new to Airbnb, they may be less likely to want to take the risk associated with a newer or lesser-ranked property. Staying with a Superhost may be a safer bet for them, and as their experience with the platform grows, they may take more risk and branch out. For a guest desiring to stay only with a Superhost, there is a tick box they can select in the search refinements to limit the search results to only Superhosts. In this particular instance, you're either in or you're out.

Airbnb Plus Status

Airbnb Plus is very different than Superhost status, and this *can* be a game changer for you if you're able to secure it. This designation is aspirational for most hosts, and there is no direct path to get there. Earning Airbnb Plus status is solely at Airbnb's discretion and is invite-only. Your property has to meet some specific requirements, be caught by the eye of an Airbnb employee, then inspected, upgraded, and finally, admitted to the Airbnb Plus program. Achieving this designates you as an elite property, which means you can earn considerably higher nightly rental and occupancy rates than otherwise comparable properties that do not have Airbnb Plus status. Airbnb Plus is the ultimate in building credibility with your guests, since they know that an Airbnb staff member has screened your property themselves, personally. Unlike Superhost status, which you should expect to receive, Airbnb Plus isn't something you should specifically try to obtain. If you're doing the right things, however, you very well may receive the invite. If not, don't fret – there is plenty of opportunity on the Airbnb standard platform and other platforms like Vrbo. In fact, if you're on Airbnb Plus, you are not allowed to list on other vacation rental sites; this is one small downside to the Plus program, but generally the higher returns you'll receive make this a non-issue.

Friends & Family

Friends and family can be a great source of referrals to your property. They can also be the non-paying guests that interfere with your profit if you let them.

Friend and family use of your property is an area we don't comment on much, because it's such a personal preference on how you share your property with this group. What we generally recommend is to set a friends and family rate. Having something prepared in advance can make these conversations much less awkward. For example, when your sister's co-worker's former college roommate asks to stay in your Tahoe property for a week during the peak season, point them to your listing, tell them to check out availability and pricing there and let them know what their discount would be from your posted rates. You can then handle any actual bookings face-to-face (off platform).

This system seems to be the least awkward; there is no expectation up front that you will let them use the property for no charge. In any case, even if we let someone use the property for no charge, we always collect the cleaning fee. This is our mandate to friends and family, and we recommend you do the same, because no matter how clean they promise to make it, your rental is your business, and you hire a professional to handle this task for a reason. In fact, even when we use the property ourselves, we always send in the cleaners afterward. Neither ourselves, nor our friends or family, has the same attention to detail as our professional cleaner. We owe it to the guests that follow to make sure the place is up to our rigorous standards of cleanliness.

Friends and family can be a great source of referrals to your property as well. No matter how big your network, it's not as big as the networks of your friends and family combined, and when a personal referral is made by a friend to a potential guest, there is a distinct credibility to it that's not always found on vacation rental sites. Furthermore, if someone books directly with you, they're likely not looking at dozens of other places before making a decision. They book with you because you've been vouched for. This is also a two-way street; you can ask your friends and family about these guests, and they will usually vouch for the guest. The result is a mitigation of risk from both sides, as well as a potential reduction in platform fees both for the guest and for the host.

Social Media & Other Marketing Channels

Admittedly, I'm not a big fan of social media in my personal life. I don't have a Facebook or Twitter account. But even I'll admit that, for business purposes, social media certainly has its place and is at this point mandatory for any business looking to reach full potential and build a brand. You can reach a large number of people using these platforms, many of whom you have some personal connection to, and you can also build significant credibility using these programs. The nice thing about using these sites is the low cost and low barriers to entry. If someone wants to book your property directly, it's also less expensive for you and for them, and you can often earn a higher net rental rate because neither you nor the guest will pay fees to a third party like Airbnb. Just make sure you have a safe way to handle these transactions outside of a mainstream vacation rental platform. Check, credit card (via Square or other program), Paypal and cash (face-to-face) are always safe plays to handle direct bookings. Which brings us to our last channel of sales and marketing...

Develop your own website. This gives you a dedicated place to point someone to learn more about your rental property and to contact you about renting it. By taking the transaction off Airbnb, HomeAway or Vrbo, it also saves you and your renter the fees from these platforms. I don't encourage you to pursue this from day one. Rather, build some history on the mainstream platforms on which you list, generate some profit and then use that to build your own site. By then, your rental network will have grown (from past guests, friends, family, Facebook and Instagram followers). Having a dedicated place for these people to book your property and only your property can be a wonderful thing.

Don't go overboard on your website. Your goal isn't to develop the world's most stellar site, as you're not trying to develop a lot of organic traffic to it. You really just want to give people who are already interested a place to go to learn more and book your property. Unless you manage a handful of properties, don't worry about marketing your website or even having it look overly professional. It should look nice, but it doesn't need to be complex. A simple Wordpress site with a real estate plugin can work wonderfully. You can take credit cards via Paypal, or if you find yourself making a lot of similar transactions, you can consider a Shopify plugin to your site. If you want to get extra fancy, you can also add a calendar to your website that integrates with your Airbnb, Vrbo and other similar calendars, but this is not always needed. You can just include links to these websites on your site and your potential guest can go there to check availability.

Of all the items mentioned in this book, having your own website is perhaps the lowest priority, so don't spend much time on this upfront. Rather, when the rental is up and running well, and you're seeing nice returns and high profitability, this is one way to help take it to the next level. The incremental returns will be pretty small, however. The other reason not to rush to do this is because taking your rental off of Airbnb/Vrbo to do direct sales may hurt your SEO placement on these sites, so make sure you have a strong listing with good history first before you head off-platform.

Chapter 8: Managing Your Guests

Operating like a Business

Managing guests is both my favorite and most hated part of operating vacation rentals. Which side it falls into on any given day depends largely on the individual guest, but fortunately I'd say 95% of the guests we've interacted with have been wonderful. Sometimes, wonderful guests simply need your help at poor times, such as when you're on vacation or a business trip, when you're dealing with family emergencies or when you're just overloaded at your day job and don't have the time to help them.

Remember at the start of this book when we talked about making sure you want to be in the vacation rental business? Once you accept that booking request, it's your responsibility to make sure your guest is taken care of, start to finish, regardless of whether they're fully self-sufficient or need the maximum amount of handholding possible, and regardless of whether you're sitting at home with all the time in the world or stuck handling your own crises.

The bottom line is that you are operating a business, and your customers have an expectation (and rightly so) that their needs will be taken care of promptly and professionally. The flip side to this coin is that, when you act like a business, you create a repeatable structure for growth. Customers love repeatability in your business and often demand it. Imaging walking into your favorite restaurant and the menu has been changed. You're a little annoyed, but it's your favorite place, so you give it a chance. You end up loving the new menu. You go back the following week, and the menu has been changed again. At this point, you'll probably just get angry. With repeat customers to your vacation rental, the same thing happens. Your renters enjoyed particular aspects about the property the first time, so they're coming back and looking forward to those things. It might be the property itself, or it might be the hosting experience you gave them, the start-to-finish local recommendations, your over-the-top friendliness as a host or a combination of many factors. Regardless of what it was that appealed to your guests, they'll expect it to be the same the next time around, and it's your job to deliver on that unwritten, unspoken promise.

There is also a tangible benefit to you for this. When you have a repeatable structure, you don't need to recreate the wheel every time you set up a new property or take a new booking. This can mean using the same check-in procedure at every property, or the same standardized response for every guest. It's a standard operating procedure that is highly scalable. This is why when you walk into a McDonalds anywhere in the country, the experience is identical. Similarly, if you hire a co-host someday, you can easily pass your operating procedures on to them. To your guest, the experience is seamless. In fact, when we use co-hosts, we *never* use the co-host feature on Airbnb. Our co-host is someone we trust implicitly, and she uses our login and password. Our guests don't even know they're talking to her because she responds as if she's us. It's seamless for the guests. While we've offered this caution already, it's worth repeating: never give your login and password information to someone you don't thoroughly trust! Operating like a business means developing and consistently following business procedures. It doesn't need not be formal, perhaps not even documented, but it should exist and be used for each and every booking you take.

Taking Care of Your Guests

We'll deal with difficult guests later, but for the easy ones, it should be quite simple for you to give your guests a 5-star experience from start to finish.

You should begin interacting with your guests as soon as they book; the sooner the better. Message them immediately after they complete their reservation, sending them a thank you for choosing your place. There's plenty of places on Airbnb, but they chose yours. Let them know you're appreciative of that and extend your help to them. I always offer to act as a mini-concierge, recommending local attractions, local hints or other things they can do to maximize their time while staying at one of our properties. I won't book anything for them like a true concierge would, but I offer plenty of advice. Always keep a list of things only the locals tend to know, such as which places are overpriced, which are too crowded and which require a reservation. It all goes a long way to making your guests happy and earning you a favorable review.

Fortunately, nearly all vacation rental sites let you save messages, and your workflow should take full advantage of this. Once you have your templates set up, sending what appears to be a customized message to your guest is simple (because it's just a saved message customized with their name or other small tweaks). I favor saving short message snippets and then stringing these together to form a full response. For example, in a hiking destination, you could save one list of all your favorite hikes, or you could save three lists: one for easy hikes, one for moderate and one for difficult hikes. You can then just grab the pieces you need for a semi-customized response. I always favor the latter approach, because my guests often ask for a particular type of hike, and I can grab what appears to be a custom message I wrote just for them, and not inundate them with useless information that they didn't ask for. It's easy for me and easy for them.

Reaching out early also lets your guests know you're adding in small personal touches to make their stay a little easier. For example, I use smart locks on all of my properties, and I always set the door code to the last digits of a guest's phone number. This nice touch shows them I'm trying to simplify their stay, but simultaneously, I'm helping ensure they don't call me because they lost their key or forgot the code. From time to time, but usually only for longer reservations or for guests celebrating a special occasion, I'll leave a small welcome card with a six pack, a bottle of wine or champagne, or some other special local treat. I use this sparingly, since it's never expected and adds to my cost. We keep all of our properties well stocked with local guidebooks, and I always let guests know to expect these ahead of time. We're often thanked because it saves our guests from buying their own copy.

Closer to check-in day (usually two or three days out), you should reach out to your guest again, if for no other reason than to give them some assurance you're ready to host them. A quick note to remind them of the check-in time, address and door code is really all that's needed. After arrival, you should check back in one more time to see if their check-in went smoothly and to see if they need any additional local advice now that they've arrived. With easy guests, this is the end of the work you need to do, and not many touchpoints are needed.

The Guest Isn't Always Right – Handling Difficult Guests

The majority of people using sites like Airbnb, HomeAway and Vrbo are wonderful people. In fact, I like to think the majority of people, period, are great. But there is a small percentage of people that can make you so overwhelmingly frustrated that you start to lose faith in humanity. Well, okay, maybe it's not quite that bad, but a bad guest in *your* home can certainly be a trying event, and it *can* make you wonder why you ever entered the vacation rental business. All hosts have been there, for various reasons, with their guests. If you stay in this business long enough, it's almost guaranteed that you will be there as some point too.

Perhaps the guest is overly demanding. Perhaps they ask you 999 questions about every little thing. Perhaps they arrived early, before you were ready for them, or demand to be able to check out late. Perhaps they broke your favorite decoration, or their children wrote on your walls with marker, or perhaps they just generally aren't a pleasant person to deal with. Regardless of the reason, managing a difficult guest just plain sucks. But remember, you signed up for this job willingly, so swallow your pride, suck it up and you can always badmouth them in their review afterwards (kidding, kidding, sort-of...).

It is always recommended that you interact with all guests (though it becomes most important when you have a conflict with a difficult guest) solely on the platform (Airbnb, Vrbo, HomeAway, etc.) where they booked. Even if the guest contacts you on your phone, follow-up with a message on the platform reiterating and documenting what was said. By doing so, you create a documented reference point that the platform's support team can use should you need to involve them. If you make an arrangement with your guests that they will pay an additional $40 to check out late but they then refuse to pay you, the support team can intervene on your behalf as long as there is written proof of your agreement. But there's nothing the support team can do if you made this arrangement verbally over the phone.

If you're experiencing a bad guest, an important first step is to understand why they're upset. Put yourself in their shoes: they just checked in, perhaps they've arrived early and the home was still dirty because the cleaner had not yet finished. Yes, it's their fault for not sticking to your posted check-in hours, but they're probably exhausted from travel, a little more ornery than usual (who isn't after air travel?) and just looking to settle in and relax. After all, that's what vacation should be. When you frame it like this, it makes it a little easier to relate to why they might be upset. In this case, the best path is to just apologize, let them know you weren't expecting them so early and remind them that you aim to deliver 5-star service every time, and that means a thorough cleaning before every arrival. *Never* go on the offensive; if it were you traveling, which would you rather hear:

1. Our check-in hours were clearly listed as 4pm; you've arrived at 2pm. The cleaner is still working, so please come back at 4 when he has finished.

2. Sorry about not being ready early; we weren't expecting you until 4pm. We had guests check out this morning, and it takes quite a bit of time for our cleaners to make sure the place is spotless for you. I know this is an inconvenience for you and you're likely tired from your travels, but if you return at 4pm, I promise the place will be spotless and ready! Some suggestions to kill the time include...

The first is very factual and isn't overtly rude, but it doesn't really do anything to help your guests out of the situation they're in at the moment. It doesn't offer them any remedies, or even show them that you empathize or can relate to their situation. The second option is much friendlier; it still reminds them (politely) that check-in time is 4pm, but it shows some empathy from you and some helpfulness from you to make some recommendations on what they can do while they wait. Importantly, neither response indicates that you took it personally (remember, this is your business; it isn't personal).

The above rather simple example defines a formula for dealing with an agitated guest:

1. Apologize

2. Empathize

3. Reaffirm

4. Offer an alternative

The first step, apologizing, is really a tactic to disarm an angry guest. It's very tough to be angry at someone who has offered a genuine apology. For many people, that's all they want, and it can stop there. Remember, never go on the offensive. A guest looking for a fight will be pretty surprised when you apologize and back down, but if you become accusatory, you'll end up giving them the fight they were looking for. Even if you win the fight, you'll lose the war when review time comes. It's worth repeating that these are *short-term* rental guests. Just swallow your pride, move on, and eventually the problem will literally go away.

The second step, empathize, shows your guest that you can relate to their situation. Even if they're completely in the wrong, do your best to understand why the situation is frustrating to them. Likely, there's an element of truth you'll discover in their side of the story. Additionally, take a good look in the mirror – *is* the guest really in the wrong? Just as sure as you'll run into a difficult guest if you stay in this business long enough, you'll also eventually goof something up. In that case, your guest has a very legitimate complaint. Getting defensive may make you completely miss the fact that the problem may be of your creation.

The third step, reaffirm, seeks to reiterate to your guest the house rules or other expectation. In the example above of the early check-in, the gentle reminder "We weren't expecting you until 4pm" is all that's usually needed to remind them of the check-in time.

Sometimes it may be necessary to escalate and be firmer in your delivery. This is, after all, your business and your property, and you have a right to control what's happening in it. If you've tried a gentle approach and it hasn't worked, a stronger reaffirmation of the rules may be warranted. But don't start there!

The final step, offer an alternative, means giving your guest the next best option that you can provide to solve their problem. Can't check out late? How about using the parking pass for an extra few hours. Can't check in early? How about recommending a few coffee shops or hiking trails they can explore while they wait. Air conditioner broken mid-stay? How about having a few fans sent over that they can use. The alternative may be enough, or it may not, but at least you're trying. For many guests, that will make a positive impression.

If you've tried everything you can do to accommodate your guest, but your guest is still just a difficult person, let it go. They'll be gone soon enough, and you can get on with your business with better guests. If your guest is actually violating your house rules though, you may seek intervention to have them removed. Your listing platform has plans in place for these events – start there. In the worst-case scenarios, you can always involve the police. In most locations (though your local laws may vary), short-term rental guests are exactly that, guests. They have no tenant rights, and you can remove them at-will with no legal eviction process. Make sure this is the case in your location before you take this action.

Chapter 9: Managing Income and Cashflow

One of your favorite parts of rental property management should be receiving income. After all, that's a large part of why you run your rental! But you're not finished once you've gotten the big payout. What you do with that money matters. Maximizing annual revenue and expenses is important to maximizing overall profitability, and maximizing profitability should be one of your main goals.

Maximizing profitability is not your only goal, however. Managing cashflow is in some ways even more important than maximizing profitability. Many profitable companies with strong top line revenues have gone bankrupt because of poor cashflow management. While you're likely not operating with the same level of liabilities of say, a typical manufacturing business (with inventory, accounts receivables, etc.), you probably do carry some debt in the form of a mortgage or other financed purchases (furniture, renovations, etc.). You likely also have major expenses staggered throughout the year, meaning you do need to be careful that you practice good cash management to avoid a situation that may leave you unable to pay the bills when they come due.

First, you should take a portion of the money you earn out of the business. Maybe not at first, but as soon as you have a stable reserve, you should be taking owner's withdrawals. At some level, this is why you start a rental business in the first place: to make money. If you're not using that money to improve your life, you're doing something wrong. We won't get into how to do that, as that's entirely at your discretion. Whether you use it to purchase more properties, purchase a new car, fund your child's college or fund your retirement is the subject of many other books and irrelevant to the topics considered here (our goal is to maximize your income, not tell you how to use it). You've worked hard to earn your vacation rental income, so you get to pick *how* to use it. But we will advise on *when* to use it. If you take every penny out of the business as soon as you earn it, you'll likely end up with cashflow problems. Good cashflow management means exercising discipline in using it.

How you manage cashflow varies with your personal goals, your location and a few other factors. For example, if you are in a highly seasonal market, you'll have periods of prosperity and periods of financial draught. This makes it more important to practice good cash management than if you're in a non-seasonal, steady rental market, since you'll need to buffer your cash reserves in order to pay the bills in the slow months. How (or if) you financed your property will also affect cashflow. If you own the property free and clear with no mortgage, it should be much easier to earn positive cashflow in every month, since most people's largest expense (the mortgage) is a non-issue for you. However, we've found that most owners experience at least one month of negative cashflow, even if the property is owned free and clear, and the usual culprit is property taxes paid once per year. This is especially true if you're in a state that requires one large annual payment and doesn't offer a monthly or semi-annual plan. This large payment can ruin that month's financials for you if you're not prepared for it.

It's important to note that cash management also varies based on your personal goals. If your goals are simply to make extra income to offset the expenses of owning your own vacation rental home or perhaps to provide additional payments towards your mortgage every month to pay it off more quickly, and if your personal budget and your W-2 income covers *all* of your rental property expenses already, then practicing cash management may not be necessary at all. You can simply take out 100% of your earnings. For most of us, this isn't the reality. Even if it is your reality, it's definitely not a path we recommend; rather, it's recommended to operate your rental property like a stand-alone business. This business should be self-sustaining and never require a cash infusion from its owners to keep it solvent (after the initial capital investment, that is). That means that, regardless of your situation, cash management should receive at least some level of your attention.

Let's consider seasonality. Perhaps your rental peaks in winter for the ski season, perhaps it peaks in the summer for beach activities or perhaps you're almost perfectly stable all year with revenue. Even if your revenue is perfectly stable, your expenses will likely not be. Perhaps your property tax bill wipes out any chance of a profit in December when it's paid. Perhaps other recurring expenses hit, like a large quarterly bill for water/sewer or your annual insurance premium. In one real world example, one of our properties has sewer, annual property tax and insurance all due in the same month. Ouch. Thanks to careful planning and good cash management, when this month hits, we just write the checks and move on. It's never fun, but also never painful.

By the time you're reading this section, your annual budget should already have been completed, and annual budgeting has already been discussed above. If you haven't downloaded the budget template already, please do so now at the link below this paragraph. Using this template, you should already have a plan for what your annual revenue and profit looks like on an *annualized* or *average monthly* basis ("Chapter 2 Planning Budget" tab). Now we'll take this planning budget and drill it down to a monthly level so we can determine our cashflow needs. In other words, the planning budget in the Excel workbook helps you determine if your rental will be profitable each year, planning for the total income and expenses you should expect to incur and helping you estimate the key financial metrics of return on cash, payback and net income. This information is valuable when making the decision to buy the property or not. The second sheet (named "Cashflow") is the next step. After you've bought the property, this sheet helps you manage the timing of expenses and owner's withdrawals to help you manage your cash to ensure you don't run out.

To download the budget sheet, please visit: **bit.ly/vacationrentalbible**

Managing cash isn't overly complicated, but it takes discipline and planning to get it right. Your budget should be your guide; with this, you should see all your known expenses laid out by month on one sheet. All your once-per-year big-ticket expenses should be easy to accurately estimate, including taxes, insurance, HOA/management fees and any other documented expenses you expect to incur. Your smaller, more sporadic expenses should be your best estimates. These expenses include replacement toiletries, miscellaneous supplies and other small repairs or items. If the timing of these expenses is a month or two off, it shouldn't be a huge issue because they're small; the key is to get the dollar amounts and frequency correct. If you have no history in your market or your property, or have never invested in a rental property before, you'll have to make some assumptions on income potential, but we've provided some tools in the previous chapters on how to estimate this already. By now you should have a good idea how to quantify your revenue.

With your completed budget, you can look at your "worst" month when you expect to realize the lowest profit. This may be due to slow revenue, high expenses or possibly both, but it's very likely there is at least one month each year when you will not turn a profit. If your budget is predicting profitability in every month, congratulations! You may not need to worry too much about cash management, but you'll likely still need to adjust your owner's withdrawals each month. If you're like most owners, you'll have one or more months of negative cashflow, offset by other months of higher than average cashflow. The main idea of cash management is to save the cash from the peak months to buffer you through the slower, negative-income months. Your budget can help you plan for this, and it can help you determine either the maximum cash you can pull out every month, or the "level-load" amount of cash you can pull out every month (which is ideal for those that prefer a steady, predictable income from their property).

Using the provided Excel template ("Cashflow" tab), you can enter all of your expenses by month. In the previous chapters, we've provided suggestions on how to estimate rental rates, occupancy rates, etc. In general, estimating revenue is much tougher than estimating expenses. We've also pre-populated the template with a real-world example from one of our earlier properties to illustrate what one real life situation looked like for us and how we managed our own cashflow and earnings.

To use the spreadsheet, navigate to the "Cashflow" tab. First input any management fee you're charged as a percentage of revenue into cell M2. If you self-manage, this is usually zero. Next, input your planned rental revenue in the green cells. You can estimate rental revenue by picking an occupancy rate and average nightly income. The rental revenue and management fee will calculate automatically. We don't factor in cleanings since renters always pay the exact amount our cleaner charges us (making it a perfect passthrough). If your situation is different for cleanings, you can add this into the rental revenue (add a row for cleaning income and add a cleaning expense under one of the "Other" expense categories).

Next, add in your expenses. You should have a good idea of most of your major expenses, and for the smaller expense items (maintenance, repairs, marketing, legal, etc.) you can take your best guess. You can update these numbers over time as you go as you learn more about your property and the expenses associated with running it. Timing is critical for the major expenses. Most of your expenses should recur monthly, such as mortgage payments, cable, internet, HOA fees, etc. Some expenses recur quarterly, semi-annually or annually such as property tax, sewer/water, trash, travel (your expenses to visit the property on a regular basis), insurance and tax preparation.

When all of your income and expenses are input, you'll see your projected gross profit per month. Look for negative gross profit numbers for each month (they'll appear in red font to help you find them quickly). These are the months when cash management is most critical.

Next, look for opportunities to make changes to your budget to smooth out the gross profit. For example, if January is showing a large loss, but March a large gain, and you're planning to pay your tax accountant in January, you may want to delay your tax prep into March to smooth out your budget. Similarly, if you have a large travel expense to visit the property, you may want to do it in a month with higher profit. A word of caution about using this approach: it may also reduce your occupancy during what's likely a peak revenue month. Maybe that fits your plans, but be aware that if your own visits are in low revenue months, you're less likely to affect your overall profitability). Finally, there are some items you simply have no control of – bills are due when bills are due, and there's no point in trying to change that.

Next, start to populate your owner's withdrawal amount. As a rough starting point, you can look at your average gross profit per month (cell P28) and enter that amount for each month. Check your cumulative cashflow and see what happens. You'll likely have some negative months. You can lower withdrawals ahead of these months and see the changes in your cumulative cashflow. The goal is to keep cumulative cashflow each month at zero or higher. Negative cashflow means you'll have to dip into your reserves to make ends meet that month, which is something to avoid if possible.

We briefly mentioned level-loading your cashflow by taking out the same amount every month, regardless of how your rental does. Some people love this approach because they want a predictable amount of income every month so they can plan their personal lives. Think of it as a Social Security check of sorts — it's fixed, dependable and simple. Level loading is likely to leave some excess cash in the account at year end, and many people we work with use this extra final withdrawal in December to fund their holiday presents. To each their own! Others we talk with prefer to take out the maximum amount they can each month without jeopardizing cashflow, and invest it in the stock market, apply it to the mortgage or invest it in another property. No matter which plan you prefer, there's no wrong answer — just the answer that works best for you.

We'll also add that we typically don't take out *all* the profit. It's our opinion that it's a good idea to maintain a strong reserve, and even when our reserve is well funded from our operating budget, adding just a little bit extra from your gross profit, even if just a few bucks per month, is a great way to offset inflation and plan for the unexpected. Perhaps we're just extremely conservative with our investments in this way, and the choice is yours on if you want to take out all of the profit or not. If you've properly allocated a reserve fund, there is no real reason *not* to take out all of the profit, so if this fits your comfort level, go for it.

Once you've developed a budget you're happy with, live by it as best as you can. But remember, the budget is a plan, and plans can (and always do) change. Sometimes you'll have a wonderful month, sometimes a terrible month. Sometimes, you'll book a long-term rental on the second to last day of the month, boosting that month's income and trashing the following month's income. Things happen that require budget adjustments, so make a plan but change it as the real world changes around you. Remember, the budget is a planning tool, not a set of instructions.

Chapter 10: Exit & Contingency Planning

The vacation rental business is fun, fast and potentially quite profitable. But it's a business, and like all businesses, your experience will include some wonderful moments of guest interaction, financial growth and prosperity, capital appreciation and learning opportunities. Similarly, you'll also experience some not-so-wonderful moments of long work hours, a part-time job you can't easily quit, guests that don't check out on time, cleaners that didn't show up, angry and difficult guests, leaky hot water heaters, broken furnishings, negative reviews, declining property values and rising HOA expenses. If you haphazardly enter the market without a plan, you may also face evictions, loan defaults, foreclosure and ultimately bankruptcy. Fortunately, if you have a solid plan then these last few items are quite rare even if your plan doesn't turn out to be fully accurate. Given the possibilities, the decision to enter the vacation rental market shouldn't be taken lightly.

Most of us have day jobs working at a company we don't own. If the business crumbles, you're out a job, but you can find another similar one at the next company without much loss. Similarly, if you just get sick of the work, you can walk away with two weeks' notice and never come back. When you manage your own vacation rental, you don't have these luxuries. You *are* the business, and if the business crumbles (bankruptcy), your financial life may crumble with it. You can't just walk away, at least not easily or immediately. You can sell the property, hire a professional manager or just stop offering rentals and turn it into a vacation home, but these take time and cost money. You should always understand the risks and the implications of entering this market before you do so.

While it's important to discuss the negatives, it's not our intent to paint a picture of doom and gloom. In fact, while it's relatively uncommon to see someone enter the market who shouldn't, it's far more common to see someone *not* entering the market who *should*. Many people we talk to say "I wish I could do that" but then never do. Some go so far as to find a property, run the numbers and then get cold feet at the last minute. Some simply assume they don't make enough money to finance a second home purchase but never walk into a bank and try. Others worry about the time commitment in self-managing while some worry they may not find renters. These are all valid concerns, and only you can make the final decision to pull the trigger. But in our experience, we haven't met many people that took the plunge and regretted it. To be sure, there have been a few of these people – generally bad investments, properties that didn't cash flow as predicted, properties with hidden damage or even couples suddenly surprised with a child and who no longer have the time for active property management. In short, life happens.

Rather than focusing on the negatives and letting those negatives talk you out of your decision, focus on the positives that can happen while planning for how to deal with the negatives should they occur. This can be a simple budgetary countermeasure to combat a specific one-off issue, such as an unforeseen major repair. Or it can be a phased or total exit plan to remove yourself from the business if need be. In fact, we encourage that everyone who enters this business have an exit plan, even if you don't expect to execute it, because you likely won't want to manage your vacation rental until the day you die. At some point, you'll want to transition out of your business, and the sooner you think about it, the easier it'll be to execute on your exit strategy when you're ready.

Your exit strategy can be staged as a progressive withdrawal from the business, or it can be a total exit strategy where you sell off the property and walk away. You can also have plans for both. A total exit plan is conceptually rather simple: list the house for sale, and when it sells, you're out of the business. In practice, it's not usually that easy. For example, it may not be a quick sale depending on the market conditions, or you may walk away with a loss even if your property has appreciated in value (due to agent's commissions and your initial investment in furnishings, repairs and renovations that may dwarf any profit you've made). But you're likely to walk away with a profit if your property has appreciated, or if you've owned it long enough for most of the initial furnishings to be depreciated off your books already and have a history of good cashflow. In fact, many people experiencing significant capital appreciation make the unexpected decision to walk away just because it's a good opportunity to realize a capital profit – either upgrading to a larger rental home, cashing out and enjoying the money or investing in something else (like a different business). We usually don't coach people to purchase vacation rentals just for appreciation, but rather to invest for cashflow. When significant appreciation happens, however, certainly don't look that gift horse in the mouth!

The thing to remember with a total exit is that you should always continue to take care of all guests you have booked until someone else has been appointed to take care of them for you (mainly, the new owner). Don't leave your guests hanging just because you're exiting the business. It's good karma and good human behavior to see through what you've started, since someone else's vacation is riding on your actions. Make the transition smooth and painless.

A staged or phased exit is a little different than a total exit, and it can take on several different forms. In its earliest stages, it is synonymous with contingency planning, and in its final stage, it may be a total exit. A staged exit can either be a response to a situation due to factors beyond your control (such as regulatory compliance), or it can be an intentional move to reduce the time you invest in your rental business.

Consider an intentional phased exit. When you first purchase the property, you may be self-managing because you're high on time and low on cash, trying to build a strong reserve fund, and wanting to really learn the business by doing all of the work. As your cash position changes (you build your reserve, refinance to lower payments or pay off the mortgage completely), you may find that your profit is growing higher and higher, and your free time smaller and smaller. At some point, your time is becoming more valuable than your profit, but you're not ready to sell your properties and call it quits. You may hire a professional property manager. This can be the first stage to exit whereby you're no longer dealing with bookings, guests and maintenance. Your profitability will decrease because you're paying someone to do work you were doing yourself already. You need to decide what's worth more: your time or your money. With your new-found free time, you can pursue other ventures – acquiring new properties, spending time with your family, working more at your day job or perhaps even writing a book on your own Airbnb successes!

Another phased exit plan could be growing your rental portfolio to include fewer but larger houses. By starting with more small, lower cost properties, you can eventually trade-up to fewer larger properties. This means fewer places to manage (although each may be more complex than a small property, generally the workload is smaller with fewer places). Perhaps you've bought two homes at $125,000 each and paid them off over time. You then have the option to trade them for a single $250,000 home with no mortgage.

Phase out by trading up; you'll reduce your own workload and get good tax benefits along the way.

Finally, regulatory concerns may drive you to execute a phased exit plan. If you're managing vacation rentals and your HOA passes a new rule banning transient rentals, you may be forced to step back to monthly rentals. For every property we buy, we ask about 100 questions that start with "What happens if…" We then look at what's going on in the local, state and national economy, and we plan accordingly. In some states, short-term rentals are still quite new, and investors are still learning how to co-exist with residents. This creates additional risk for the investor. If the investor's business model relies on short-term rentals to cash flow (a situation which everyone reading this book is likely in), and legislation eliminates the short-term rental market, your business plan can flop very quickly without a backup plan. A well-prepared investor will know their financial situation for their second (any maybe third and fourth) best course of action. This contingency plan can then be executed readily should such a situation arise. Such a plan might include conversion from short-term to a monthly vacation rental, or to a long-term rental, or even selling the property. If you know what your options are up front, and have the budgets done already, you'll be much more prepared for a quick reaction than anyone else in your area, and you'll get a first-to-market advantage when you have to execute on your backup plan.

Conclusion

Managing a vacation rental is rewarding work, both personally and financially. To repeat what we said in the introduction – it's not a get rich quick plan, but rather a stable platform for long-term income growth. But as you've seen from either reading about it here or taking the plunge already, it's a road filled with hard work, highs, lows, happy surprises and unforeseen mishaps. For some, purchasing and managing a vacation rental is the key to financing vacations; for others, owning personal vacation properties in favorite locations may be the goal. For others it's purely a business – perhaps just the first of several they may start. No matter how you use or plan to use your property, we hope you are now better equipped to understand the needs you will face as the owner of not just a property, but a budding business.

If you haven't taken the plunge yet and bought your first property, I hope this book has helped you understand what will be required of you should you choose to proceed. It's rather easy, at least in that it's straightforward and formulaic. But it's also a significant amount of work and can be time consuming. I hope the tools that have been provided, especially the budget templates, are being well utilized by you to evaluate a few potential properties. I hope you and your realtor or other investment partners are using these tools well to analyze a variety of properties.

We spent a lot of time discussing strategies to evaluate profitability, write compelling copy, furnish your property, take great photos, boost organic SEO, earn 5-star ratings and manage cashflow, but I'd like to close with the gentle reminder that, although I've encouraged you to operate like a business, never forget that behind this business are humans, on both sides of the transaction. Take good care of your guests. You may never meet them, or even talk to them, and they may never be able to pick you out in a lineup, but I guarantee your guests will always recall the home away from home you've provided them during their trip along with the memories they made and the comfort they felt having a great place to sleep every night. Similarly, you as the host are only human; you'll make mistakes and learn from them, but if you're persistent and learn to weather these storms, you'll find yourself building a wonderful vacation rental business that provides a nice, stable cash stream for years to come. Good luck!

Glossary of Terms

Acquisition Costs – The all-in cost to purchase a property. In addition to the purchase price, acquisition costs can include inspection costs and closing fees.

Capital Budget – A budget that evaluates potential major projects or investments, such as acquiring the property, improving the property or furnishing the property.

CC&Rs – Formal covenants, conditions and restrictions placed on a group of homes or condominium complex by a builder, developer, neighborhood association or homeowners association.

CPA – Certified Public Accountant.

Depreciation – A reduction in the value of an asset with the passage of time, particularly due to wear and tear.

GAAP – Generally accepted accounting principles are authoritative standards and the commonly accepted ways of recording and reporting accounting information.

HOA – A homeowners association is an organization in a subdivision, planned community or condominium that makes and enforces rules for the properties and their residents.

Operating Budget – The operating budget shows projected revenue and associated expenses for an upcoming period. For the purposes of a rental property, this includes ongoing maintenance expenses such as cleanings, replenishing toiletries and replacing or repairing broken or damaged items.

R&Rs – Rules and regulations set by HOA board members and applicable to a group of homes or condominium complex.

Reserve Study – Long-term capital budget planning tool that identifies a stable and equitable funding plan to offset ongoing deterioration, resulting in sufficient funds when those anticipated major expenditures actually occur.

Return on Cash – The annual return the investor made on the property in relation to the amount of cash invested into the property during the same year.

Sunk Cost – Money that has already been spent and that cannot be recovered.

Made in the USA
Coppell, TX
11 August 2021